Buffalo Soldiers
in
Arizona

BUFFALO SOLDIERS

— IN —

ARIZONA

JOHN P. LANGELLIER

THE
History
PRESS

Published by The History Press
Charleston, SC
www.historypress.com

Cover images: *Front*: The circa 1880s caption on this photograph reads, "Corporal Edward Scott, 10th U.S. Cavalry. Shot by Apaches at Sierra Pinito, Mexico, May 3rd, 1885. Thigh amputated May 8th, 1886. Operator: Paul R. Brown, M.D." *Courtesy Otis Historical Archives, National Museum of Health and Medicine, CP 1855, OHA 75 Contributed Photographs Collection*; by the early 1900s, Charles Young, third Black graduate of West Point, had risen to the rank of captain with the Ninth Cavalry. A few years later, he reported to Arizona as a major with the Tenth Cavalry. *Courtesy United States Army Heritage and Education Center*; besides cavalry and infantry assignments, Black soldiers served in support roles, including in the quartermaster corps, the branch in which this salty sergeant, with his civilian Colt revolver, served in the 1920s. *Courtesy the author*; an infantry company from the Ninety-Second Division smartly marches out as it trains for the Second World War. *Courtesy United States Army Heritage and Education Center*. *Back*: Indian scouts and handpicked troopers from the Tenth Cavalry formed a formidable strike force, led by Lieutenant Powhattan Clarke. During the 1880s and early 1890s, they pursued Geronimo and other Apaches resisting reservation life. *Courtesy Freeman's-Hindman Auctions*; the Ninety-Second and Ninety-Third Infantry divisions prepared for overseas duty during World War II at Fort Huachuca. *Courtesy United States Army Heritage and Education Center*.

First published 2025

Manufactured in the United States

ISBN 9781467157094

Library of Congress Control Number: 2024947469

Notice: The information in this book is true and complete to the best of our knowledge. It is offered without guarantee on the part of the author or The History Press. The author and The History Press disclaim all liability in connection with the use of this book.

To Eileen, "My Shining Starr."

"History, despite its wrenching pain, cannot be unlived,
but if faced with courage, need not be lived again."
—Maya Angelou

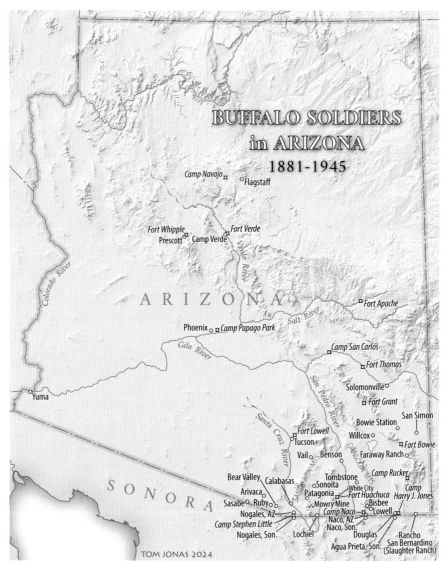

Map of Arizona and northern Sonora, with highlights of key Buffalo Soldier locations, 1881–1945. *Courtesy Tom Jonas.*

CONTENTS

Acknowledgements

The following organizations and individuals contributed to this volume:

ORGANIZATIONS
Arizona Historical Society, Tucson, Arizona
Armed Forces Institute of Pathology, Washington, D.C.
Bisbee Mining & Historical Museum
Fort Huachuca Museum
Frontier Army Museum, Fort Leavenworth, Kansas
Greater Southern Arizona Area Chapter Ninth and Tenth Horse Cavalry
    Association
Henry F. Hauser Museum, Sierra Vista, Arizona
Hindman-Freeman Auctions, Cincinnati, Ohio
Library of Congress, Washington, D.C.
National Afro-American Museum and Cultural Center, Wilberforce, Ohio
National Archives and Records Administration, Washington, D.C., and
    College Park, Maryland
National Museum of Health and Medicine, Silver Spring, Maryland
National Park Service
United States Army Heritage and Education Center, Carlisle Barracks,
    Pennsylvania
United States Military Academy Library, West Point, New York
University of Arizona Libraries, Special Collections, Tucson, Arizona

INDIVIDUALS
John Covington
Katie Horstman
Donna Jackson-Houston
Tom Jonas
Bryan Jones
Robert Pickering, PhD
Shaun Rodgers
Daniel Smith
Eileen Starr

I also am in debt to the late Dr. Blaine Lamb, who suggested I follow his example and publish this study with The History Press. In the process, my able acquisitions editor, Laurie Krill, and the editorial team at The History Press deserve credit for their efforts enabling the completion of this title. Finally, Robert Bluthardt and Stephen C. Gregory provided invaluable assistance without which this project would not have been possible. Despite extensive support, all errors, omissions and statements made in this publication are the sole responsibility of the author.

"Traditional Home of the Buffalo Soldier"

ORIGINS

From colonial times through the American Civil War and after, Black patriots have fought for a country that often treated them with little or no respect. Nonetheless, since the 1960s, historians and assorted authors have paid considerable attention to the exploits of the so-called Buffalo Soldiers. The exploration of African American U.S. Army personnel in Arizona, however, has been treated in scattered studies. A statewide perspective, such as the titles by Monroe Billington for New Mexico and Nancy K. Williams for Colorado, does not exist. Admittedly, a few others have focused on aspects of this rich story, as evidenced by several titles cited in the bibliography. Yet a broader treatment of African American soldiers in the Copper State, from the 1880s through the mid-1940s, remains to be published.

BLACK MILITARY EXPERIENCE IN ARIZONA

Building on these previous studies and weaving together local history with a broader context and the larger narrative of the Black regulars offers fertile ground for a more comprehensive exploration of this significant aspect of American history. A review of race relations between the Black soldiers and Arizona's multicultural, multi-ethnic population along the borderlands

deserves attention, as does chronicling the diverse roles played by Black soldiers in Arizona from their entry into the territory in 1881 through the eve of World War II.

Among other features worth contemplating was Arizona's distinction, shared with Texas and California, that all four of the regiments from the 1869 reorganization act served in the territory and later state. The missions of these regiments often overlapped or repeated themselves, as did successes and failures. So, too, did interactions with local communities, typically consisting of whites and Latinos. For the most part, these contacts proved positive, especially through the performances of Black military musicians along with frequent sporting events.

While the Second World War remains a worthy topic, so, too, do two nineteenth-century African American West Point graduates, Henry O. Flipper and Charles Young. Both spent time in Arizona, albeit in the former case, he did so as a civilian. Additionally, both of the first Black soldiers to receive commissions by promotion directly from the enlisted ranks, John E. Green and Benjamin O. Davis Sr., reported to the state during part of their distinguished careers.

Finally, as with most states in the trans–Mississippi West, prior to the United States' entry in World War II, the percentage of Black residents fell below the national average. The presence of African American troops significantly added to the overall Black population.

Opposite, left: The first African American graduate of West Point, in 1877, Henry Ossian Flipper received a commission as a second lieutenant in the Tenth Cavalry. *Courtesy U.S. Military Academy Library.*

Opposite, right: Charles Young, the third and last nineteenth-century African American graduate of the U.S. Military Academy, served part of his distinguished army career at Fort Huachuca. *Courtesy National Afro-American Museum and Cultural Center.*

Right: Benjamin O. Davis Sr. obtained a promotion from a squadron sergeant major with the Ninth U.S. Cavalry to receive a commission as a second lieutenant. He would retire a brigadier general, the first Black soldier to obtain this grade in the U.S. Army. *Courtesy United States Army Heritage and Education Center.*

YEAR	BLACKS	WHITES	APPROXIMATE %	COMMENTS
1940	14,993	499,261	3.0%	World War II strength increase begins after 1941.
1930	10,479	435,573	2.4%	Black troops stationed in U.S./Mexico border.
1920	8,005	334,162	2.4%	Black troops stationed in U.S./Mexico border.
1910	2,009	204,345	.98%	Most Black troops did not return to Arizona until after 1911.
1890	1,357	88,243	1.53%	First Black troops were stationed in Arizona, 1885–98.
1880	155	40,440	.038%	No Black troops were stationed in Arizona.[†]

YEAR	BLACKS	WHITES	APPROXIMATE %	COMMENTS
1870	26	9,938	.26%	No Black troops were stationed in Arizona.
1860	21*	2,421	.87%	Arizona totals as part of New Mexico Territory; 4,040 Native Americans.
1850	8	820	.98%	Population of Tucson included 87 Native Americans.

* Free Blacks.

† According to the 1880 U.S. Census, there were 155 African Americans in Arizona, most of whom (76) lived in Pima County. By 1893, that number had risen to 1,357, the major increase stemmed from the posting of African American troops in the territory. *Sources*: James W. Yancey, "The Negros of Tucson, Past and Present," unpublished MA thesis, University of Arizona, 1933, 13–14; and Alton Hornsby Jr., ed., *Black America: A State-by-State Historical Encyclopedia* (Santa Barbara, CA: ABC-Clio, 2011), 37.

CHAPTER 1

NINTH CAVALRY

"WE CAN, WE WILL"

ORIGINS

This regiment came into existence by virtue of an Act of Congress approved on July 28, 1866. Designated the Ninth U.S. Cavalry, the first man enlisted, George Washington, joined on August 5, 1866. Many of those who followed Washington's lead had been enslaved. Among them were numerous Union Civil War veterans who had served with the United States Colored Troops. After a brief formative period in the vicinity of New Orleans, the new unit headed west to Texas.

Thereafter, the Ninth Cavalry served in the Lone Star State and elsewhere, carrying out diverse missions ranging from duels with formidable Native Americans to the removal of white interlopers from Indian Territory (Oklahoma) intent on seizing portions of the reservations granted to numerous tribal people. Elements of the Ninth also deployed to Colorado and New Mexico Territory. In the latter instance, Black cavalrymen attempted to keep order during the so-called Lincoln County War that boosted William "Billy the Kid" Bonney's notoriety. Furthermore, the regiment participated in a relentless campaign against the intrepid Mescalero Apache leader Victorio. This elusive, tenacious tactician and his followers kept the U.S. Army at bay through the late 1870s until his death at the hands of Mexican troops on October 14, 1880.

Dapper Sergeant E.D. Gibson stood for this circa 1880 studio portrait in the field uniform of the type worn in Arizona during the Nana campaign. *Courtesy Frontier Army Museum, Fort Leavenworth.*

With Victorio's passing, the venerable Nana, who likely was an octogenarian, took up the fight. In July 1881, Nana with fifteen warriors, the remnant of Victorio's band, reinforced by about twenty-five Mescalero Apaches, reentered New Mexico from Chihuahua. They plundered and killed a number of settlers in the territory, according to an unpublished regimental history.

To worsen matters, Arizona Territory erupted in violence that continued through the mid-1880s and beyond. Nana and other Apache warriors kept the military at bay. Reinforcements arrived in Arizona to quell the threat. The first known Black troops were included in this escalated effort to bring about peace. Anton Mazzanovich, a native of Croatia who had enlisted in the U.S. Army, reported that these additional horse soldiers made their way from Fort Wingate, New Mexico.

This was Company I, Ninth Cavalry, which during the summer of 1881 took to the field. Company I's incursion into Arizona was the first known official entry of the Ninth Cavalry into Arizona. This was far from the last time, however, that elements of the regiment reported for duty in the territory. On October 2, 1881, Company F, Ninth Cavalry, commanded by Captain Henry Carroll, arrived at Willcox from Separ, New Mexico. They came aboard a special train at 7:00 p.m. In due course, Company F rendezvoused with Captain George A. Purington's Company H, Ninth Cavalry, and ultimately formed part of a successful engagement against the Apaches.

In an atypical instance of a multiracial strike force consisting of white troops from the First and Sixth Cavalries, Yuma Indian scouts and the two companies of the Ninth Cavalry, the combined column managed to accomplish another rare feat. They closed and met an enemy who usually bolted when confronted by a superior force. As Private Mazzanovich recalled:

> *The two colored troops were ordered out to pick up the trail. Everybody went to work with a will. It took but a short time to load, as we led our horses on the platform of the freight house and thence into the box cars. In the way of provisions, we loaded four boxes of hardtack.*

All the cavalrymen, both Black and white, operated under orders to "unload at the Dragoon Summit" and from there to "head toward the Old Mexico line, in an effort to cut off the Indians and keep them from getting over into that country also to prevent them from entering in Cochise's stronghold west of us," wrote Mazzanovich.

On October 4, the two companies of the Ninth overtook the Apaches, who might have been one hundred strong in addition to their women and children. Nana and the others halted to confront their pursuers. At 2:30 p.m. on October 4, 1881, the Buffalo Soldiers approached the South Pass of Dragoon Mountains. The advancing Ninth cavalrymen drew the first enemy volleys as they struck the Apaches' rear guard.

The determined Apache defenders employed this effective tactic in order to allow the women, children and the elderly to escape. A running fight of about fifteen miles followed. It lasted until sundown. The Ninth attempted to block the Apaches from escape into Mexico, but to no avail.

Previously, Private Mazzanovich noted that as he passed a "large cottonwood tree I observed two of the colored troopers lying close to it. It looked as if they had been wounded and were out of the fight." Not far away, he espied a dead Apache woman with "a little Indian girl, about six years of age…crying over the body."

Another contemporary account from the time added, "One Indian girl, about eight years old, was taken prisoner. She was richly dressed, and is supposed to be a chief's daughter." Likewise, the October 6, 1881 edition of the Las Vegas, New Mexico *Daily Gazette* noted that "three colored soldiers were wounded." These were Private William Carroll with a minor gunshot injury to the thumb and two more severe cases for Privates James Goodlow (wrist and hand) and Henry Harrison (leg). Besides the three men, the patrol had a wounded horse. With that, the Ninth Cavalry left Arizona to take up duties elsewhere in the United States and, during 1898, in Cuba.

RETURN TO ARIZONA TERRITORY

After the regiment returned from Cuba to the United States, late in 1898, the veterans of the Ninth entrained to Arizona. Once again, the twelve troops were scattered to several outposts. Late in the following year, the Ninth had responded to new orders. For instance, Troop A assumed detached service from Fort Grant to build a telegraph line from San Carlos to Dunlap's Ranch. In another instance, Troop F, under veteran Victorio campaigner Captain Henry H. Wright, with forty men headed to Naco to suppress troubles on the Mexican border.

The ruckus resulted from a scuffle between an American and a Mexican in Naco, Sonora. After the former knocked down the latter and started back to the United States, Mexican police responded. In the process, a shot from an unknown source triggered armed Mexican responders to appear from all quarters. *Gringo* cowhands quickly added to the scene. An account from the Arizola, Arizona *Oasis* added that a bystander from the United States, Dan Burger, while attempting to board a nearby train, "fell with a bullet in his left leg." The same article mentioned that Mexican guards sustained serious wounds, while another innocent bystander, a British citizen named James Ryan who was unloading freight for the Cobre Grande company, likewise became a victim. During the indiscriminate shooting, Ryan's body was "said to have been riddled with bullets."

In the aftermath, two Americans caught in the fray, a cowboy named Joe Rhodes and George Marts, employed in the Mexican community, both became prisoners in Naco, Sonora. Rowdy American cattlemen threatened to rescue the pair from the jail. Their threats went unfulfilled. Mexican authorities dismissed Rhodes. Marts, however, briefly remained in custody.

The arrival of Captain Wright and troops from the Ninth Cavalry, along with the dispatch of a Mexican colonel to confer with the U.S. officials regarding the matter, ended the troubles. The October 31, 1899 edition of Phoenix's *Arizona Republican* noted, "Saloons on the Mexican side are responsible for the disturbance." While it was more complex than this explanation suggested, one fact stood out. Military authorities correctly credited the "appearance of troops and the judicious action by Captain H.H. Wright 9th Cavalry, their commander," with preventing further violence.

Fortunately, more peaceful exchanges between the locals and Black soldiers usually prevailed. Indeed, interactions between the two groups could be cordial. For instance, the formation of a baseball team at Fort Grant helped cement good relations. The players proved popular enough to be considered for a tour to Bisbee, Tucson, Phoenix and Congress. A proposal, according to another piece in the *Arizona Republican*, suggested a plan for games that "could be arranged in such a manner that each town visited would bear its portion of the expense." The soldiers' ability to play ball, the reporter contended, "would be an exceptionally good drawing card," as would the fact that many if not all of the team members had served in Cuba, where the regiment "rendered such undeniable assistance to the Rough Riders."

This period of affability proved short-lived. Gradually, elements of the Ninth departed Arizona for other locales, including the Philippine Islands. By early 1901, no unit from the regiment remained in the territory.

THIRD DEPLOYMENT TO ARIZONA

More than a dozen years and several deployments in the United States and abroad ensued before the Ninth Cavalry headed back to the newly admitted state of Arizona. In 1912, the regiment's reappearance resulted from the conclusion of strong man Porfirio Díaz's decades-long stranglehold on Mexico. His departure left a power vacuum that ignited a long-simmering revolution.

News of the regiment's return to Arizona engendered mixed emotions. Often, when communities learned that Black troops were to be stationed in the area, fear arose that trouble would follow. Military records, however, demonstrated that crime rates among white and Black regiments tended to be equal.

Unfortunately, when the advance party of the Ninth Cavalry appeared, trepidations surged. The day the first troops of the Ninth arrived, the *Bisbee Daily Review* recounted the visit of some troops to the "restricted [red-light] district," where the men "proceeded to raise a rough house with the inmates of the houses there." Two Douglas law enforcement officers responded. When they confronted the revelers, one of the troopers brandished a pistol after he and his fellow rowdies had been warned against disturbing the peace. Both officers unholstered their sidearms. In response, the rest of the cavalrymen with "the party then drew and the officers very wisely 'put up.'"

Rather than pursue the matter, the pair withdrew to avoid bloodshed. Following the first encounter, Arizona's governor, George Hunt, responded to a request from Douglas's mayor and others. Hunt addressed a message to the regimental commander, Colonel John Guilfoyle, with a request to restrain his men and avoid future clashes. The colonel complied. Additionally, orders prohibited troops from carrying firearms into town.

For the most part, that pattern was not the norm in Arizona. As an example, in response to the first disorderly behavior, Phoenix's *Arizona Republican* contended that the "offensive conduct" stemmed from "the boisterousness of a few of the rougher soldiers, possibly inflamed with liquor. Few such outbursts, however, marred the regiment's reputation."

RACE RELATIONS

Indeed, members of the Ninth Cavalry band enhanced good military community relations in Douglas, Tombstone and other sites in southern

Arizona. In Douglas, during late September 1912, schoolteachers received a treat when "at 8 o'clock the Ninth Cavalry band rendered a concert of seven numbers which were greatly enjoyed, each number receiving hearty applause." The rather eclectic program included Rollo Chapi's *Spanish March*, Wagner's *Tannhauser* overture, *The Chocolate Soldier* by Strauss and four other offerings.

Afterward, a *Bisbee Daily Review* reporter added that the band moved to the venue's veranda, where "dancing started and lasted until the early morning hours. Society turned out in great numbers and most of the officers in command of the Ninth cavalry were present and introduced to the citizens." Refreshments completed the evening, served on the lawn in front of the Douglas Country Club, which was illuminated by Japanese lanterns.

Every afternoon, educators and others enjoyed free music. For a brief period, Ninth Cavalry bandsmen offered "a short concert" during the daily change of the guard. Further, during the summer, on many Sundays, they appeared at the city park for the pleasure of the local citizenry. The popular players also performed for political rallies. Likewise, they appeared in patriotic parades during appropriate holidays. As examples, "the famous" Ninth Cavalry Band joined two Elks' lodges in Douglas for the Flag Day Parade, where the band headed up the march. During Bisbee's 1913 Independence Day celebrations, troops from both the Fifth and Ninth Cavalry regiments paraded behind the governor and his party aboard automobiles and schoolchildren in other motorcars.

The growing popularity of automobiles also allowed out-of-town visitors to head to Douglas and observe the Ninth Cavalry soldiers firsthand. During July 1913, that was what a group of Safford motorists did. Guests from other communities likewise came to Douglas, where they could enjoy the military musicians. In September 1913, Douglas's fraternal organization, The Eagles, invited their counterparts from Bisbee to join them for "Music, Dancing and Much Else." To this end, the Douglas Aerie (chapter) engaged the Ninth Cavalry band to greet their friends on arrival at the train depot and later at a brilliantly lit venue for "a big barbecue and vaudeville entertainment." Later in the day, the orchestra of the Ninth Cavalry furnished dance music.

The Ninth's bandsmen even serenaded the Mexican Consulate in Douglas. Some five hundred *Constitutionalistas*, one of several vying rival groups in Mexico, took offense until they found that the band had been engaged by a Mexican tailor who paid for their services. With that, the "excitement then abated," or so indicated Tombstone's *Epitaph* for September 21, 1913.

Ninth Cavalry bandsmen had to be accomplished equestrians and proficient musicians, as demonstrated by their appearance in Douglas's Fourth of July parade, 1913. *Courtesy the author.*

Moreover, at another southern Arizona setting, the charming Ramsey Canyon southeast of Fort Huachuca, the Ninth Cavalry's orchestra enlivened dances. There, the tunes wafted "in the open air over a running brook and under walnut and sycamore trees." The unit offered comparable performances at the Warren District Country Club along with the previously mentioned Douglas Country Club, including a booking in September 1914 when the gala season opened with the Ninth Cavalry musicians providing the entertainment under the baton of their noted bandmaster, Wade H. Hammond. In July 1915, Hammond's musicians returned to the country club for the directors' ball at "one of the most delightful affairs given this season." Later that month, as the July 10 issue of the *Army and Navy Register* indicated, "the officers and ladies of the 9th cavalry entertained their army and civilian friends at one of the most elaborate affairs given in Douglas since the coming of the troops. The pavilion was most profusely decorated, the 9th cavalry band furnishing the music."

In 1895, Alabama-born Hammond graduated from that state's Agricultural and Mechanical College. After graduation, he made his living as both a musician and as a tailor. Soon thereafter, he performed as the bandmaster at his alma mater and later at Western University, from which he joined the Ninth Cavalry in 1909. His regiment sent him to the Royal Military School of Music in London at its expense, which permitted him to travel to other countries. After two months, Hammond returned to resume his position as bandmaster with the Ninth. A Cheyenne, Wyoming newspaper championed him as "the most accomplished negro musician in the service." A few years later, while the regiment resided in Arizona, the mayor of Douglas presented Hammond "with a gold medal set with diamonds." This medal, purchased by popular subscription, expressed "the gratitude of the citizens for the services of the band during the last two years." It bore as part of the inscription, "Keep step to the music of the Union." Over a decade later, Hammond was still serving at Fort Huachuca, where he had become one of the first Black warrant officers. He continued to be a popular figure there and throughout the Southwest. Under his baton, the Ninth gave regular concerts in Douglas at the city park with impressive programs, according to the September 4, 1915 edition of the *Chicago Defender*.

On a more solemn occasion, newly arrived Douglas resident Nellie Suydam Cowley witnessed "a military funeral" in which the deceased comrade received final honors from the Ninth Cavalry band mounted "on horseback." The band played the "Death March" while "the soldier's horse was led behind the hearse covered with black."

In addition to bands bringing soldiers and civilians together, sports initiated similar interactions. In but one example, the Douglas Country Club fielded a baseball team. Its nine matched bats with the officers from the Ninth Cavalry. When they met, the regimental hospital corps attended, supposedly "to take charge of any player who knocks a homerun and faints from exertion or surprise; or has a stroke of apoplexy when he foozles the ball; or has his face stepped or when stealing a base."

Periodically, a team composed of enlisted members took to the field, where they faced civilian opponents, including a matchup in Bisbee's Warren Park against the Warren District Grays; at another time, they bested the Pearce smelter workers. According to Bisbee's *Daily Review*, "The Ninth Cavalry team is considered to be one of the best teams in the state." Occasionally, "picked teams" of soldiers "from Troop B and C Ninth cavalry" provided spectators with "a snappy and interesting game." During another soldier-versus-soldier matchup, "The 12th infantry ballplayers, who last Sunday crossed bats with the 9th cavalry boys at Douglas, were badly beaten by their colored brothers, the score being 4 to nothing." Although the national pastime dominated, football occasionally pitted soldier-players against civilian opposition. The C. & A. Smelter's football team practiced "every day…at noon, commencing Monday, for the game with the 9th Cavalry, November 21." At other times, such as in July 1915, the Ninth Cavalry's nine participated in a "well played" matchup against the Eleventh Infantry in a competition that portended integration. The Eleventh bested the Ninth, winning 8–5.

COMBAT READINESS

Members of the Ninth sometimes participated in public demonstrations other than sporting events. For instance, according to the *Arizona Republican*, during early 1914, representatives of both the Ninth and Tenth Cavalry regiments competed in a rifle match with civilian participants. Requests from the Arizona State Fair in Phoenix also requested Captain Theodore Schultz furnish a detachment of the Ninth. Schultz, "on account of the educated high school horses, which he owns," was sought after as an attraction at the fair. These well-trained mounts had won a number of prizes at different horse shows, as well as entertained an audience at Douglas on the July 4, 1913, about which a Bisbee reporter extolled, "The exercises which they were put through were most astounding. Besides being beautiful animals, they are perfectly trained and keep perfect step to music. They are equal to the best trained circus horses and their appearance would be a distinctive feature of the event."

Similarly, in Naco, Arizona, residents gathered to witness the annual Russian Ride, where several troops from the Ninth Cavalry "stationed at the border city participated in the drill." Supposedly, this equestrian test was "one of the most difficult of the riding feats which the cavalryman is called on to perform in the course of his duties." The relatively small civilian audience at the ride applauded

Officers favored polo. During July 1912, four of them from the Ninth Cavalry won this trophy, presented by the Douglas Chamber of Commerce. *Courtesy the author.*

"the candidates as they completed the difficult test." The occasional polo match also drew citizens, but only officers indulged in this fast-paced horseback contest.

At other times, elements of the Ninth Cavalry conducted field maneuvers, including one where they "camped over night at Warren, while on a 6-day hike from Douglas to Fort Huachuca and return." On this outing, they pitched their tents and picketed their horses opposite the baseball park. At another time, Troop C, Ninth Cavalry, "stationed at Naco made a practice march to Bisbee." The men briefly remained and "then returned to camp." Combat readiness, however, required more than horsemanship and field exercises. Periodic target practice, which in one case revealed that among the enlisted men "about twenty-five percent of the total were improving," remained essential. Enhancing the ability to deploy for war required more than physical training. From the Civil War through the 1866 reorganization act and beyond, military regulations provided for a unique position during the era, that of regimental chaplains who would minister to the rank and file in units with African American personnel.

MILITARY INSTALLATIONS

Further, the army provided medical care to its troops. One of the doctors serving these needs pronounced the overall health of the Ninth as good,

Troops from Ninth Cavalry encamped in Douglas, as seen here in May 1915. Later, the community became the site of Camp Harry J. Jones. *Courtesy the author.*

yet the impending winter concerned him. During the first year in Arizona (1912–13 season), cold weather presented new challenges. At Naco, troops set aside strictly martial duties to construct "winter quarters, which is taken to indicate that they intend to be comfortable." Troops B and C set to work "erecting an adobe barracks building" of sufficient capacity to house both troops. The soldiers furnished all the labor, "including digging of adobe material and baking of same," in order to replace disagreeable tents over the winter with improved living quarters that would offer "plenty of warmth."

The next year, similar activities in Douglas resulted in the transformation from what was a tent city to a substantial settlement of adobe structures. To enhance these mud brick dwellings, improvements were envisioned such as the planting of flowers and the edging of streets lined with whitewashed stones.

Efforts to prepare more permanent, improved living conditions arose from increased troop numbers. Among them was the Ninth Cavalry, with its troops relocated from Nogales to Douglas. Soon, twenty-two troops of cavalry spread out across southern Arizona; ten troops of the Fifth Cavalry, newly arrived from the Philippines, gathered at Fort Huachuca, which expanded to accommodate the regiment including a new railway line.

To maintain that readiness, the Ninth Cavalry received "the best equipments of any stationed along the border at this time." Supposedly, "Uncle Sam is good to his soldiers and provides them with the best to be had including the food they eat, the clothes they wear, and tents that houses them and the wood they burn."

As further evidence of the Ninth Cavalry's settled status in the region, they completed "building a big amusement hall out of a barracks." With strict segregation prevailing throughout the nation, provision of a place where the men might enjoy entertainment was not a mere gesture, given that Black troops could not avail themselves of many public facilities such as movie theaters. Acceptance of Black troops by the white populace went only so far.

One of these theaters in Douglas screened motion pictures, including a controversial film *Birth of a Nation*, based on the popular novel *The Clansman*. Attuned to the fact that "some friction here between the white and colored troops already" existed, Nellie Cowley envisioned "that if the play were brought here it might cause riots." She approached the Douglas Women's Club to discuss the matter. She "knew there were a good many Southern people here," but their attitude surprised her. In brief, the majority of the club members supported the film being played "regardless of what trouble it causes."

SOLDIERS OLD AND NEW

While public entertainment might be segregated, a recruiting office opened in the area for both Black and white candidates. This was not the only option to apply for enlistment or reenlistment. Vance Marchbank, who previously "completed his first hitch (three year enlistment) and had already served at Fort Robinson, Nebraska, and Fort Crook, Nebraska… reenlisted the second time March 1, 1899." Upon returning to the duty, Marchbank reported to Troop L, Ninth Cavalry, which "was then stationed at Fort Huachuca, one of the few water holes established when the west was young which is still in existence." Of the more than four decades he claimed as a soldier, Marchbank spent 1899, 1913–17, 1920–21 and November 1923–February 1932, approximately thirteen years, at Fort Huachuca along the Mexican border.

Marchbank was not alone in his long years with the army. As a matter of fact, the regiments with Black soldiers tended to have a high reenlistment and retention rate. First Sergeant J.A. Jones, Troop I, Ninth Cavalry, provided a prime example of the many men who made the army a career worth pursuing. After decades of faithful service, he retired on a $67.50 monthly pension "for the balance of his life." Moreover, "During his many years' service Sergeant Jones has been economical and saved a considerable sum of money," which would allow him to purchase a modest home after he returned to Baltimore, Maryland, where he and his family would reside.

He spoke positively of his days in uniform, which he "enjoyed…fairly well, and always been on duty, having seen but few sick days in my life. I remember that eighteen years ago I was somewhat tired of the service and on the verge of quitting the army, it being time for re-enlistment." An officer encouraged Jones to remain in service. He indicated, "I took his took his advice and remained, and today I am thankful." He went on to praise this captain and the regimental commander, Colonel John Guilfoyle. Jones maintained that Black troops never "had a better friend among the white people" than the colonel. At the end of his interview, the veteran of San Juan Hill surmised, "It will be news to many people to know that after thirty years' service in the United States army even non-commissioned officers and privates can retire on a permanent pension."

BENJAMIN O. DAVIS SR.

Retirement was but one reward for faithful service. Advancement in the military brought other incentives. Enlisted personnel, usually after considerable time, could rise to the position of senior noncommissioned officers or even obtain a coveted, infrequently available slot as a staff NCO in several of the support branches such as ordnance, commissary and quartermaster departments. On exceptional occasions, promotion from the ranks to obtain a commission occurred for a few white soldiers and a remarkable pair of Black sergeants who came up through the ranks. Benjamin O. Davis Sr., the best known of the duo, made the transition from an ambitious Ninth Cavalry squadron sergeant major to a second lieutenant in the same regiment. In 1901, Davis passed the required examination "with honors, averaging 91 percent." Once he surmounted this hurdle, an African American–owned paper predicted that his success would "greatly encourage the negro soldiers who have not heretofore believed it possible for one of their race to get into the regular establishment as a commissioned officer."

During World War II, as seen here at Fort Huachuca, Brigadier General Benjamin O. Davis Sr. made visits to Arizona, where he sometimes inspected the troops. *Courtesy National Archives and Records Administration.*

Moreover, another publication under Black ownership, the *Colored American*, optimistically indicated, "Yes, the soldier white or black, who appears before an Examining Board physically and mentally unqualified will be turned down. We have in the service who will be able to do just what Mr. Davis has done if they get down to study. The door is open, who will be next?"

The newly minted shavetail's first assignment was to the Tenth Cavalry. Four years later, he advanced to first lieutenant. In that grade, Davis reported to Liberia as the U.S. military attaché through November 1911, when he returned stateside. Eventually, during Franklin D. Roosevelt's administration, Davis not only became the first African American promoted from the ranks to a commissioned grade, but he also accomplished another first as the beginning of a long line of Black officers in the U.S. Army to don the star of a brigadier general.

While William Vrooman never gained the fame achieved by Brigadier General Davis, this stalwart veteran "completed his thirty years' service in the United States army…receiving his discharge from the Ninth cavalry, in which he served during the entire time. Vrooman enlisted in the year 1886 at Buffalo, New York, when he was 16 years old," or so the *Copper Era and Morenci Leader* from Clifton, Arizona, indicated in the September 17, 1915 issue. Although Vrooman was underage at the time he joined the military, his official service record in other ways paralleled many a faithful enlisted man who made the Ninth Cavalry his home. After enlisting on June 18, the newly enlisted private would be assigned to Troop I, Ninth Cavalry, on January 22, 1887. By September 17, 1889, he had risen to sergeant in the same troop.

Late the following year, he spent several months in early 1891 as a member of the force sent to Sioux country. As the *Copper Era and Morenci Leader* went on to share, he "[p]articipated in an engagement against hostile Indians at

Drexel Mission December 28, 1890" and, several months later, received his honorable discharge dated June 17, 1891. After a typical leave of absence between "hitches," he returned to duty, reenlisting on July 10, 1891. His new assignment to Troop G, Ninth Cavalry, as a private again resulted in Vrooman's appointment as a sergeant, effective on April 17, 1892. Over the next three years, he displayed his prowess with the revolver, earning a number of medals during competitions as well as a distinguished marksman award (the highest qualification in the army) in 1894.

Vrooman later served in Cuba during the Spanish-American War, including in battle at Santiago de Cuba. Between September 16, 1900, and September 16, 1902, he saw duty in the Philippine Islands, where saw action in "numerous engagements with insurgents in the Provinces of Albay and Camarines." He would return to the Philippines from May 31, 1907, to May 15, 1909. While there, on January 22, 1908, he became a squadron sergeant major. Then, on January 1, 1909, he reached the top of his career as an NCO when he was appointed regimental quartermaster sergeant for the Ninth Cavalry.

The *Copper Era* article ended with a testament that applied not only to Quartermaster Sergeant Vrooman but that also might be said of many of the long-serving Buffalo Soldiers: "His loyalty to his duties was unwavering even under the most trying circumstances."

Another longtime NCO, Troop A, Ninth Cavalry's "top kick," left the military under very different circumstances. Some of his friends stated that First Sergeant Sam Kioney's rabbit foot brought him luck. Kioney "received word that he had fallen heir to considerable property." Perhaps a few of the individuals in the area envisioned that Kioney would share some of his newfound wealth. For certain, the presence of the Ninth Cavalry, along with all the other units stationed in southern Arizona, brought economic benefits.

Even lumber became a much sought-after commodity. "They say the soldiers are getting all the wood in the country," related Nellie Cowley. Some of the wood was destined to finish "building a big amusement hall out of a barracks." The traffic became so prevalent that she and her spouse considered putting up a fence to impede the "detachments of United States army trails through our back yard." At least the cavalry had not as yet "taken to cutting across" their property.

In spite of these sorts of inconveniences, the boon to local business, and other aspects of the Ninth Cavalry's presence along the border, promoted a degree of positive attitudes in Douglas and elsewhere in southeast Arizona. For one thing, Douglas's chamber of commerce expressed a positive attitude to the regiment. The organization went so far as to contact its Congressional representative, Carl Hayden, "to use his every influence with the war department to have the Ninth cavalry permanently located here." Many in the community appreciated "their presence and regard them as permanent residents of the city." This was in contrast to a great number of places in the United States where Black troops were unacceptable. That was not true in Douglas, where the opinion of the chamber concluded that "a better behaved lot of Negroes were never assembled in any community than those assigned here." Another echoed this: "The soldiers, who are a well-behaved bunch, proud of the uniform the wear, and at all times respectful to civilians." Previous trepidations and "ill-feeling over the presence of the negro troops here, since some disorders shortly after the regiment's arrival" apparently gave way to a better opinion of the Black cavalrymen. By 1913, one newspaper reporter maintained that the idea that "the colored troops would cause trouble [was] unfounded."

Besides acknowledging the positive performance of most of the cavalrymen from the Ninth out of "[h]umanity, justice, enlightenment and patriotism," another factor entered the equation: an "ineliminable element of material interest, have conspired to bring about this altogether to be desired condition. The troopers themselves seem fully to realize that upon their proper conduct depends their stay in the vicinity of Douglas; and right well do they live up to a standard and deport themselves that render their presence innocent of anything savoring of the disagreeable."

ECONOMIC IMPACT

Also, the reality that soldiers spent a certain portion of their pay in the area made them more acceptable. Regular visits from the army paymaster at Fort Huachuca to Ninth Cavalry troops along the border brought considerable cash, given that the amount of $13,000, in one instance, represented a significant boost to the area's economy. The young, newly arrived soldier John P. Campbell provided a firsthand account of the process. After an unsuccessful effort to enlist at sixteen, two years later, inspired by family members who served before him during the Spanish-American War, he returned to the recruiter. This time, at eighteen years old, Campbell went from Jefferson Barracks, Missouri, to Fort Huachuca. Soon after joining the Ninth Cavalry there as a private, Campbell reported for border duties, as well as was occasionally detailed "to help pay the troops." According to Campbell, "We'd ride to the fort in a buckboard and get the money. The pay was kept in a small safe, with a driver, and an officer, and two guards riding the wagon while two other guards rode horseback.'" Several days and several stops ensued to deliver the money to the men "who were scattered at the outposts."

Although pecuniary motives existed, more than financial reasons likely prompted seasonal good wishes from the Warren District Commercial Club. During the holiday season of 1914, the organization extended "a cordial invitation to the soldiers and officers, in camps on the border." It offered "in a spirit of true comradeship. The celebration, which still gives promise of being held, will be a Mecca for the United States troops and they are welcome, according, to all of the signs of the times and the declarations of the residents here."

CRIME, VICE AND PUNISHMENT

How genuine these expressions of hospitality were cannot be ascertained. What can be deduced is that in some instances relations between the civilian population and Ninth Cavalry personnel became strained. To this point, not every soldier, regardless of skin color, enjoyed the same good will in the borderlands. As Rudyard Kipling observed in his 1890 poem, "Tommy," "Single men in barracks don't grow into plaster saints." Some Black soldiers in southern Arizona fell into this category, to the disdain of numerous locals and fellow soldiers alike.

Ninth Cavalry private John King found himself in the jail, in his case for forgery. Somewhat akin to King's wrongdoing, Joseph Burch, a trooper of the Ninth Cavalry, stood trial "charged with procuring a false affidavit." Others succumbed to liquor, a fate that placed Private Hamilton from the Ninth Cavalry in hospital after being "thrown out of a buggy in which he and two others were returning to the camp at Naco." Once released from medical care, he transferred to a branch of the county jail, where he spent a night, presumably due to drunk and disorderly conduct, and the next day appeared in court, where the judge fined him ten dollars and costs, a considerable sum on a thirteen dollars per month.

Also, Private McAllister Weden's over-imbibing ended with local law enforcement taking him into custody for disturbing the peace. Following Weden's arrest, "four other soldiers demanded" the prisoner's release. After the officer "refused and started to walk his man down the street," the four soldiers made a run for him. He "drew his revolver and ordered the soldiers back. The sight of the big 38 Colts brought a ready response to the order." Then the officer telephoned for backup. They arrived in time to take the inebriated soldier into an automobile and drive him to the police station, where, after a night in custody, his court appearance resulted in a $7.50 fine for disturbing the peace.

Troopers Luther Cooper and Walter Brewster of the Ninth Cavalry were sober when they "stole $34 in money and his jewelry" from a local mining man, who later identified the pair of thieves. Regimental officers turned over their larcenous subordinates "to stand trial for highway robbery." The following month, Copper and Brewer, after they entered plea of guilty to larceny, received sentences of one to five years each.

Other offenses committed by or against Ninth Cavalry personnel also went to court, resulting in incarceration, the gallows or no punishments at all. For one thing, rumors of Black American deserters from the U.S. Army crossing into Mexico and serving as soldiers of fortune made sensational reading, albeit such tales emerged from scant or erroneous evidence. Some of these accusations proved accurate, at least when it came to Corporal James Shields of Troop L, Ninth Cavalry. Shields's superiors charged him "with many varied crimes." Specifically, they contended that the corporal held two of his comrades "at the point of a pistol and relieved them of their rifles and revolvers." With weapons in hand, he slipped across the border "into Mexico and was received with open arms by the rebels. They at once made him a captain and gave him command of a company of barefooted and big hatted soldiers." He made one error. Shields returned north to visit his wife. Once back on U.S. soil, his discovery led to apprehension followed by the guardhouse.

Mostly minor infractions dominated, although far more serious crimes existed. For instance, Private John Stuart faced charges for criminal assault, which resulted in imprisonment. A second trooper, Allen Sanders, faced charges for assault with a deadly weapon. At the same time Sanders appeared in superior court, one more Ninth Cavalry enlisted man, Louis Nelson, pleaded not guilty to murder charges.

On payday, Nelson of Troop E stole a rifle from camp, made his way to the Cooper City Club in Douglas and entered the saloon. Stepping inside, he fired at another member of the regiment, Albert Jones, who died from his wounds. A stray shot also struck the club's piano player, Tom Evans, leaving him severely wounded.

Soon, Policeman Robert Hart entered the scene and Nelson surrendered to him. Nelson stood trial. After hearing the evidence, the jury concluded Nelson was guilty and imposed the death sentence. Nelson could stand when the judge addressed him and confirmed that the defendant was to be hanged.

Because "certain testimony that was not admitted" but "should have been," Nelson was transferred from the state penitentiary to Tombstone for a retrial. Upon review of evidence not presented in the first hearing relative to Nelson receipt of a death threat whereby the killer contended he acted in self-defense, the county superior court called for another trial. Instead of the death penalty for murder, the jury found Nelson guilty of manslaughter, which brought a minimum of ten years imprisonment.

Similarly, Robert Thompson, Troop M, Ninth Cavalry, faced judgement "without bail, to answer to the charge of murder in the killing of his comrade, Edward Smith at the cavalry headquarters in Douglas." On the morning of August 25, 1913, the pair of Ninth Cavalry privates quarreled over a wash basin. Military witnesses, four officers and ten privates, took the stand either for the prosecution or the defense. The evidence against Thompson also ended in his sentence of ten years' imprisonment, which after review was upheld.

Another incident of death at the hands of a fellow Ninth cavalryman involved John H. Landes and Wilbur C. Griffin, both from the machine gun platoon of the Ninth Cavalry. The circumstances noted that Griffin provoked Landes, which led to a general fight in one of the tents. Landes stabbed Griffin with a knife that entered the victim's "brain through the forehead." Like Nelson and Thompson, Landes "claimed that he was acting in self defense." The court-appointed defense, Landes being without means, prevailed.

In all three cases, the adherence to due process proved the norm. This record contrasted with widespread lynchings, particularly in former slave states. For example, in 1913, fifty Black citizens and only one white citizen died at the hands of vigilante actions. Of further interest, in Arizona, between 1882 and 1968, a total of thirty-one individuals died at the hands of the mob, but none of them was Black.

Even a matter that could have provoked retribution at the hands of locals received its day in court. Ninth cavalryman John Stewart "criminally assaulted two little colored children below Lowell, a couple of weeks ago, entered plea of guilty." His "particularly atrocious" offences against a seven- and an eight-year-old drew "an indeterminate sentence of from five years to life" rather than ending up dangling from a rope supplied by an angry mob.

Adherence to legal procedures also applied to homicides other than those that erupted between soldiers. Indeed, sometimes soldiers perished at the hands of civilians. This was the fate of Sam Franklin, a packer with the Ninth Cavalry whom James Moore, "better known as the 'China Kid' because of his peculiar slanting eyes," slayed early in 1914. The rivals quarreled "over Georgia Conley, a comely mulatto woman of doubtful character," or so stated the *Arizona Republic*. Moore countered that "he had to stab Franklin" to save himself and evidently Conley, both of whom "were badly bruised and battered." Apparently, the physical damage convinced authorities to release Moore without charging him.

Mary Watson was not so fortunate. She appeared before the Superior Court in Tombstone, where she pleaded guilty to manslaughter. Why she killed Private John C. Norwood remains a matter of speculation. Regardless of what motivated Watson, she "received an indeterminate sentence of from one to ten years in the state penitentiary."

While only speculation exists in terms of what prompted Watson to kill Norwood, a Private Williams of the Ninth Cavalry inflicted a fatal wound on himself for a discernable reason. He committed suicide from "anger at being jilted by a woman with whom he was in love." Enraged by his rejection, Williams shot himself on the street in downtown Douglas.

Clear-cut motives also induced fairly recent arrivals to Troop B, Ninth Cavalry, Charles Dingle and Ben Merriwether, to slay thirty-five-year-old Armando Hernandez. They intended to rob the chauffer, and according to a later report, they thought to use the money to desert after arriving at Naco, where they had easy access to Mexico. The victim resided in Douglas for ten years with his spouse and two children. He provided for the family by driving an automobile that shuttled soldiers and other to and from their destinations, an essential service during an era when access to vehicles remained scarce. Hernandez's occupation cost him his life. W.P. Tester of Douglas found Hernandez "[l]ying with his head in a pool of blood at the side of the road by his Hudson car…murdered a mile the other side of Forest Station." Tester telephoned law enforcement. Officers immediately set out solve the case and bring those responsible to justice.

They quickly located their suspects, Dingle from Aiken, South Carolina, and Merriwether, a native of Augusta, Georgia. After their arrest, the pair underwent separate interrogations. Each of them "broke down and confessed the murder, though each puts the crime upon the other." The assailants revealed that they had hired Hernandez to drive them to Bisbee. In transit, they shot the driver, who "pitched forward, his head going through the windshield, and being badly cut. The bullet entered the small of his back," probably causing instantaneous death. Dingle alleged that Merriwether formulated the plan and fired the pistol that felled the ill-fated driver. Merriwether offered opposite testimony. The only detail they agreed on was that they assaulted Hernandez "shortly after leaving the Douglas camp Saturday evening at dark." They claimed to have knocked down him down, but he "raised an outcry and scared [them]" so they fled.

Actually, it appeared that "they lifted the body out and threw it on the ground." They pulled Hudson well off the road, which meant "no one noticed it until after nightfall." Then they walked back to camp after not finding any money on the dead body, or so they asserted. Before doing so, they used a military overcoat to mop up the blood in hopes that it would appear the driver died from a crash. This bloody overcoat served as one of two of the pieces of evidence used to convict them. The other was Merriwether's uncleaned pistol.

The pair "waived examination" and were held for "superior court without bond." As they had insufficient funds, a court-appointed attorney defended the culprits. He failed to obtain an acquittal, and they faced the consequences. The judge called for the death sentence and set the date of Friday, June 4, for a dual hanging at the state penitentiary in Florence. This appointed date came and went. A parole and pardon board met to review their sentences along with four other applications related "to condemned murderers for commutation of sentences from death to life imprisonment." Their reprieve soon ended. On February 6, 1917, Arizona's Supreme Court denied their appeal. Nevertheless, previously on December 16, 1916, the state had banned executions. Because the death penalty would not be reinstated until December 5, 1918, they remained behind bars awaiting their deaths. Even then, the two former cavalrymen never mounted the stairs to the gallows.

Although violent crimes and other infractions occurred, like occasional desertions, such events tended to be aberrations. In fact, for the most part, the men of the Ninth Cavalry in Arizona ably performed their diverse duties. During the period prior to World War I through the early 1920s, the regiment especially undertook assignments that, after the Labor Appropriation Act of 1924, would become the responsibility of the U.S. Border Patrol. In fact, the one of the U.S. Border Patrol's predecessors, the U.S. Immigration Service (formed in 1904), concentrated on enforcement of border crossings with special attention to restricting Chinese immigration under strict, discriminatory legal quotas of the era. Black regulars played other important parts along the long, often tempestuous boundary between Mexico and the United States.

BORDER DUTIES

One of the regiment's priorities involved the interdiction of an array of smuggled, prohibited or restricted commodities, from armaments and ammunition to drugs and liquor, in particular mescal. Their preliminary entry into this unfamiliar realm ended unsatisfactorily. To begin with, one of the first actions involved detaining a vehicle of presumed arms' smugglers. Pulling over the suspect, who actually "had been away on a hunting trip," the trio of sportsmen met a patrol that halted them in the vicinity of San Bernardino Ranch. The Ninth Cavalry detachment believed they had stopped the illegal traders. "The party suggested that John Slaughter," the nearby ranch owner, "be called on to identify them and testify to their good characters, and this was done." Legendary "Texas" John Slaughter "arrived, declared he knew them, and that they were who and what they had represented themselves to be. Then there were friendly farewells, and the party resumed its homeward journey."

A few months later, a detail from the Ninth Cavalry made a second unsuccessful effort that entailed a raid on a Douglas hotel. A squad of troopers from the Ninth Cavalry and four officers attempted to seize "Joaquin Esquiera, supposed to be a rebel leader," in spite of "protests of the proprietor of the hotel who demanded a search warrant. Allegedly, Mexican secret agents supported by the cavalry contingent "entered the hotel and searched twenty-three rooms." Although Esquiera was not on the premises, the hotelier was. After the abrupt intrusion, he claimed that the raiding party assaulted him. His statement led Tombstone law officers to issue warrants for the arrest the Ninth Cavalry force and the Mexican secret service. In response, the regimental commander, Colonel Guilfoyle, supposedly responded that his orders called for the apprehension of "any rebel leaders found on American soil."

The following year, 1913, Ninth Cavalry troopers and several agents of the Mexican government failed to secure "several hundred ammunition boxes at the rear of the Douglas Hardware Company's warehouse. Reportedly each box contained 1000 rounds of ammunition," but upon examination, the crates were empty. Conversely, men of the Ninth fared better when they captured A. Dalton, who, while poised at the border, "had in his possession a .30-.30 rifle and 200 soft nosed cartridges." A Ninth Cavalry patrol halted Dalton. They "asked him his business and whither he was bound." His fabricated reply indicated that he "was sheriff of this county," but the officer in charge personally knew the sheriff. Dalton altered his story, claiming to be a colonel in the Mexican army. Finally, when taken into custody, "he made a third statement saying he was a prospector going into the Patagonia mountains, but he was headed for the Ajo mountain. After so many misleading statements and counter-statements, the soldier of fortune was led to the Ninth Cavalry guardhouse. Without a formal complaint against Dalton, and with a lack of sufficient evidence, the military confiscated his goods and discharged him from custody.

At another time, the Ninth failed to halt contraband ordnance from reaching Mexico. Remarkably, ten thousand stolen cartridges from Ninth Cavalry ordnance stores avoided detection and crossed "the international line without the knowledge and connivance of the soldiers." Yet the Ninth Cavalry succeeded in interdicting arms' smuggling. One of these efforts ended in the imprisonment of "nine Yaqui Indians who had in their possession a big lot of rifles and ammunition which they were smuggling into Sonora." These would-be arms gun runners "were chased from across the Mexican line by customs guards but were unable to escape our Uncle Sam's boys." Later, "two prisoners charged with attempting to smuggle munitions of war were brought in by U.S. soldiers," greatly strengthening border security. Thereafter, the Yaqui captives remained in custody of the U.S. troops. Despite being charged with "smuggling arms and ammunition into Mexico," they would not be released "to the Mexican authorities." Instead, reportedly, they were "to be detained indefinitely by the American soldiers."

Later, troops from the Ninth took two other suspects into custody, a pair of Douglas residents, Isadore Illitzy and W.E. Schwamm. The men "waived a preliminary hearing and were held to await the action of the Federal grand jury." While they awaited the convening of the grand jury, they each posted a bond of $500. Although not discovered actually smuggling, they had the ammunition in their places of business when raided by special agent of the Department of Justice and troops of the Ninth Cavalry. The agent, with the support of the troops, confiscated the ammunition and placed the perpetrators under arrest. These actions constituted a more aggressive, "new interpretation of the neutrality laws making it an offense to handle contraband munitions of war," even though they never delivered their forbidden haul to Mexico.

It was not just contraband items that resulted in action by patrols from the Ninth. Individuals including "Juan Castillo, a commissioned officer of the Mexican state troops was arrested Saturday morning…for violating the neutrality laws by attempting to deliver important messages" to his contacts in Naco, Sonora.

In some respects, these assignments combined latter-day duties assumed by the FBI and the U.S. Bureau of Alcohol, Tobacco and Firearms, as well as to the greatest extent missions performed in the twenty-first century by the U.S. Customs and Border Protection. It was this last task that constituted the major need for the Ninth Cavalry and other U.S. Army units dispatched to southern Arizona. Since the 1912 Marts and Rhodes affair that brought elements of the Ninth Cavalry back to Naco, a community that straddled the U.S./Mexico border, fighting to the south between Mexican central government forces and revolutionary elements regularly threatened residents living near the explosive war raging from Chihuahua to Sonora. These contests not only caused concern in Naco, Arizona, but also affected other border communities in Arizona as far west as Yuma and to the east in portions of New Mexico.

IN HARM'S WAY

As in other matters, Bisbee's *Daily Review* carried stories that revealed Mexico's multifactional feud, which affected life north of the international boundary. For instance, on September 12, 1912, the paper published a typical revelation: "Reports from Douglas say that our neighbor on the border is putting on military airs again. With the ninth cavalry…on this side of the line and with something like eight hundred Mexican federals, including four hundred Yaquis Indians in Agua Paleta, the Douglasites should feel secure from harm." Two days later, the September 14, 1912 edition of the *Arizona Republican* added, "The entire Ninth cavalry, commanded by Colonel Guilfoyle with the exception of one squadron troop, is encamped here [Douglas]. The colored troops are to be used to patrol the border from Douglas east to the New Mexican line." Part of these peacekeepers served under squadron commander Major Herbert White, who detailed one of his two troops to John Slaughter's San Bernardino ranch and the other to Naco.

The Ninth Cavalry's detail to the Arizona-Sonora line between the two nations went beyond symbolism. After 1910, with the abrupt forced departure of Porfirio Díaz, a power vacuum fractured Mexico. When Díaz stepped down, Francisco Madero became president. His Constitutionalists gained their power base in the main from Mexico's urban areas, mainly in the center of the country. Emiliano Zapata, another leader, occupied southern regions with the support of Indigenous people, while Pancho Villa gained prominence in the north backed mostly by ranchers and miners.

General Victoriano Huerta's successful coup placed him in the presidential palace, as well as included the overthrow and assassination of President Madero. In opposition to Huerta and his Federalists, the Constitutionalists, also known as the *Carrancistas* (so named because of one of its chief figures, Venustiano Carranza), rallied. Zapata and Villa joined Carranza intent on Huerta's overthrow. Sparring between the two factions spilled over into the United States.

On one hand, unintended results periodically unfolded north of the border. Occasionally, the Carranza "rebels" intentionally acted "to force intervention by the United States." Whatever the circumstances, by early 1913, arrangements for the Ninth Cavalry "to greatly strengthen the border patrol between Douglas and Naco" constituted one of the first moves by the United States in light of rebel raids in the vicinity of Naco, Sonora, relatively close to the Mexico/United States line. Strikes on ranches to procure "mules, food supplies, blankets, and ammunition" prompted a reaction by the federals in the manner of the dispatch of Colonel Emilio Kosterlitzky and his *rurales* to Agua Prieta opposite Douglas. Although federal forces were on hand, "the looters were unmolested." Adding to the volatile mix, the threat of "a mutiny of the federal garrison at Agua Prieta" increased concerns for Douglas and provoked an alert of four troops of the Ninth Cavalry.

By March 1913, passive observation had given way to a clash between presumed Mexican forces and men of the Ninth Cavalry. Four officers from the regiment received fire from the Mexican side. Sixteen troopers rushed to support their superiors. A running fight followed. The U.S. patrol killed a half-dozen Mexican soldiers, with many wounded. In turn, "None of the American troops was killed or wounded." The advance party held their positions until reinforced by Troops E and F, Ninth Cavalry. "The American troops became so excited that they overstepped the boundary and pursued the Mexicans for some distance. The fight caused great excitement at Douglas. The townspeople armed themselves and rushed to the boundary, believing that the Mexican soldiers were intending to invade the United States."

The wounded, along with the dead, supposedly were not "a detachment of Mexican troops crossing the border." Instead, one source asserted that they "proved to be a party of Mexicans gathering with pack animals." In contrast, the official military recounting of the thirty-minute engagement against Mexican regulars reported that the United States troops fired an estimated two thousand rounds or more. The Mexicans returned fire with as many shots. In this account, "Neither side crossed the international line." Instead, they blazed away separated by three hundred yards, "with the International line between them."

To preclude a recurrence of skirmishing, Colonel Guilfoyle mobilized almost the entire regiment, including the machine gun platoon. The show of strength sent a message that the gringos could defend against any eventuality. Also, the colonel forwarded a report to his superiors in Washington. One newspaper article claimed that Guilfoyle's brief contained "a copy of a message which was found in the possession of the arrested Saturday from the Maderista Junta in which there was a plan outlined for a union of the rebels on the Mexican side with those on the American side. It is said the plot was to attack Douglas and Aqua Prieta at the same time." This inflammatory Mexican missive, which predated the notorious "Zimmerman telegram" of World War I, purportedly contained "violent anti-American statements."

These varying versions of the exchange characterized the barrage of accusations and counteraccusations made by American and Mexican representatives, which the front-page headline of the March 5, 1913 *Arizona Republican* summarized: "Both Sides Say Others to Blame for Outbreak." Regardless of fault, once again, elements of the Fifth and Ninth Cavalry regiments responded, especially after another clash that took place in Nogales left Deputy U.S. Marshal A.A. Hopkins wounded by a stray bullet fired from Mexico. Hopkins would not be the last bystander on U.S. soil to fall victim to fighting from the Mexican side, which additionally prompted an estimated ninety Yaqui troops accompanied by twenty-five women and children from the federal forces to desert and hand themselves over to a captain from the Ninth Cavalry at Naco, Arizona. That number quickly rose so that soon "the Ninth cavalry had 216 of the former soldiers…besides some fifty women and children" who crossed into the United States. One reporter wryly speculated that "it is barely possible that some of the deserters have been attracted by the elaborate culinary department of the Ninth cavalry."

An ultimatum from the United States that Mexican federal troops "must cease firing, in the case of attack, when the signal was given him" supposedly was backed by a threat that the Ninth would "cross the line if their order is disobeyed." In such an eventuality, Troops I and L with the machine gun platoon reinforced Naco, thereby increasing the complement to "eight troops of United States soldiers there, four short of a regiment." Additionally, a twenty-man escort accompanied a wagon load of ammunition sent from Douglas as increased supplies for the growing Naco command.

The sprawling tent city that sprang up in Naco, Arizona, housed the Ninth and Tenth Cavalry regiments during the Mexican Revolution. *Courtesy University of Arizona Library Special Collections.*

While the drama unfolded, regimental colonel John Guilfoyle dispatched six troops to Naco and among other things placed the post's "old two-story adobe theater building in condition to shelter the Yaqui Indian prisoners in case a battle should occur at Naco." He housed the Yaquis on the second story and reserved the lower story for a shelter to protect "the women and children of Naco which Col Guilfoyle declared would be forcibly taken out of danger" if the contingency became necessary.

Regarding obeying orders, the two squadrons posted to the area closely observed activities across the border to prevent the shooting of Americans "by keeping them back from the danger zone." Seemingly, patrols on the roads leading to Naco had orders to warn "Americans to keep back from all dangers." Others guarded "business houses in Naco to prevent looting or disorder" should fighting erupt between the Mexicans, which, in due course, it did.

In early April 1913, beleaguered Mexican federal troops under Pedro Ojeda faced their long-expected enemies nearly a mile below Naco. Despite precautions by the U.S. military, during the three-hour exchange "bullets sprayed the American side, and wounded four negro troopers of the Ninth cavalry and one army teamster." As the result of "two distinct battles during the day and a continual long range artillery duel, the federals…lost 40

Camp Naco, Arizona, stood but a rifle shot away from the U.S./Mexico border. *Courtesy University of Arizona Library Special Collections.*

wounded and 7 killed," while the count for their Constitutionalist opposition led by Victoriano Huerta and Álvaro Obregon, remained unknown at the time. Of these "[t]wenty wounded federals...brought...for treatment by the United States army medical corps, two died while in the hospital."

They would be joined by Private White, who while on patrol duty received a wound in the hand and leg. In turn, his comrade Trumpeter Fleming was struck in "the shoulder, the ball piercing his body and falling into his blouse pocket." Another Black cavalryman, C.J. Brown, "was shot in the abdomen while in camp," which greatly reduced his probable survival.

Routed mainly by determined Yaquis, who bore the brunt of the Constitutionalist assault, many of General Ojeda's men fled. Remnants of Ojeda's "federal garrison of 300 troopers in Naco, Sonora, surrendered to the United States troops on border patrol...after having withstood a siege of state troops which lasted for five days, and in which more than half of his command was killed." The general himself nearly fell or would have become a prisoner had it not been for Troop A's commanding officer, Ohioan Captain Herman Augustus Seivert. The Ninth Cavalry officer "ran alone to his assistance." Dashing to the rescue, "He grasped the Mexican general by the arm. Together they ran in a hail of lead to where an automobile was waiting."

During this time, one report speculated that Ojeda had succeeded in his efforts because he possessed "artillery of the latest French pattern, throwing two explosives a minute." The guns' lethal effect was credited to "Englishman, John Dean, an expert marksman," who directed "the artillery fire...assisted by two American negroes, deserters from the Ninth cavalry." The veracity of the last statement can be challenged, although similar claims periodically appeared in print.

Dean probably avoided capture, as did the Mexicans who had surrendered to Ninth cavalrymen at Naco. By April, they no longer enjoyed sanctuary. The Americans repatriated them, meaning they marched the men across the line. The Ninth Cavalry responded to similar orders to "dispose of all soldiers held at Nogales and Naco" with the exception of General Ojeda.

Even so, the administration in Washington expressed its relief after the warring parties ceased the contest for Naco, Mexico. Realizing that a possible renewal of hostilities existed, Brigadier General Tasker Bliss,

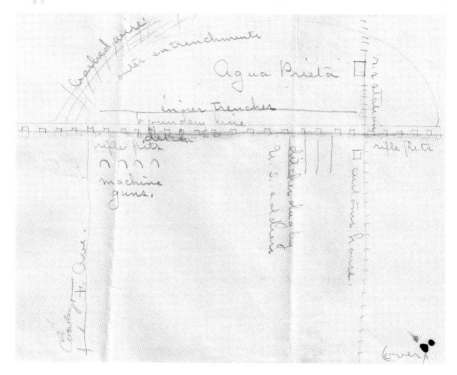

Nellie Suydam Cowley's sketched this diagram of the Ninth Cavalry, depicting the entrenchments manned by troopers from the regiment in 1915. Their defensive positions came about as the result of a major clash between rival Mexican forces that erupted south of the border in Agua Prieta. *Courtesy the author.*

commanding the United States border troops, "warned the combatants that further firing into American territory would not be tolerated, but the Mexican commanders had a hard task trying to keep their volleys directed away from the border."

Good intentions aside, a few months later, rounds from Federalists discharged from their "entrenchments at Naco" Mexico struck on the United States' side of the line. This action restarted the conflict, which Nellie Cowley mentioned to her mother: "I see that Villa is bearing down on Agua Prieta. I hope that he captures it and get the battle over. I hear, however, that the U.S. troops have orders not to tolerate any such action as took place at Naco."

She further shared that the upsurge of American forces in the area totaled "four and two-thirds regiments of infantry...and one of cavalry and the Sixth Field Artillery." Resembling World War I in Europe, they dug "intrenchments facing the line" bolstered by sandbags.

These defenses offered only partial protection, as evidenced by Private Howard Wilson of Troop B, Tenth Cavalry, being shot. Soon after that, Private Leroy Bradford of the same troop was added to the casualties on the American side of the line, along with several horses. Wilson and Bradford

At Naco, Arizona, U.S. cavalrymen pressed metal breastworks along with a network of trenches as makeshift protection against rounds that occasionally came across from Mexico. *Courtesy University of Arizona Library Special Collections.*

Massive stacks of haybales bespoke of the need to feed large herds of livestock that were used by the troops posted along the border, but they also provided another barrier against stray bullets fired from Sonora. Buying this fodder and others purchase by the army brought economic benefits to many communities in southern Arizona. *Courtesy University of Arizona Library Special Collections.*

were only two of many Ninth and Tenth Cavalry enlisted men who fell victim to wild rounds from Sonora. By October 11, a pair of Ninth Cavalry privates required medical treatment.

Others experienced close calls. During an October fracas, although no fatalities resulted, a member of the Ninth cavalry had his hat shot off. Some of this soldier's comrades were not as fortunate.

Once again, Naco became a battlefield, this time under Pancho Villa's surrogate, José Maytorena. By noon of October 14, another four Black cavalrymen as well as three civilians went down from bullets fired from Sonora. Of these cavalrymen, Private Robert B. Watson, Troop A, Ninth Cavalry, suffered a stomach wound that rendered him the only fatality. Likewise, the prognosis appeared to dire for Private Daniel Wakefield, Troop E, Ninth Cavalry, who sustained a hit to his temple. Both Sergeant Nathan Stitch and Private Ponce McCarver incurred leg wounds. Watson and Wakefield went to Fort Huachuca for surgery. A second report added that Wakefield probably would be totally blind but had "a fair chance of recovery," as Bisbee's *Daily Review* postulated on October 18, 1914. Nearly

The Mule Mountains stood as an impressive backdrop to Camp Naco, Arizona, when it still was a temporary encampment for Ninth and Tenth Cavalry troopers who lived under canvas. *Courtesy University of Arizona Library Special Collections.*

two years passed before Cleveland's *Gazette* printed on May 13, 1916, a fairly complete list of eighteen soldiers struck by stray bullets during these events in 1914.

Apprehension based on these events prompted preparations for immediate field service. This included the cancelation of all leaves by the Ninth United States Cavalry, along with soldiers of that regiment preparing their equipment and taking charge of "several carloads of extra wagons received…at Douglas." With that, transportation capable of hauling supplies for one thousand men over a six-month campaign became available.

In early February 1914, a brief respite resulted from President Woodrow Wilson's "proclamation lifting the embargo against the exportation of arms into Mexico." With that, the Ninth Cavalry headquarters "withdrew the border patrols under their jurisdiction along the international boundary" that prompted them to strike "their camps along the border and assembled at the general camp, one mile outside of Douglas."

The short-lived break from field service soon ended. Just a few weeks later, "The Ninth cavalry and also the Tenth…again resumed close patrol on the Border." Their return to the international line was meant to prevent "violation of the neutrality laws through the passing of armed bodies of men" from the U.S. side to the aid either the federals or the rebels on a

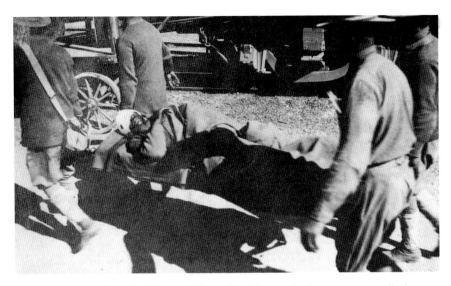

In 1914, casualties from the Ninth and Tenth Cavalries required transport to medical facilities. *Courtesy University of Arizona Library Special Collections.*

During 1914, ten men from the Ninth Cavalry and eight from the Tenth Cavalry sustained wounds inflicted by stray bullets from Sonora. Among them, one Ninth Cavalry trooper died, and another was blinded for life. *Courtesy University of Arizona Library Special Collections.*

comparatively far-flung front. Once again, elements of the Ninth Cavalry stretched westward to Yuma and eastward to New Mexico. In the last mentioned statement, a skirmish occurred indicative of ongoing friction and potential escalation between the many groups gathered at the border.

These deployments temporarily put to rest gossip that some of the cavalry patrols along the Arizona border would be withdrawn and transferred to Texas. Resurrecting border patrols was not without drawbacks. A bold raid supposedly by Constitutionalists, now styled *Huertistas*, to abscond with some of the Ninth Cavalry's coveted machine guns made the news. The plunderers were from the Ninth Cavalry's camp a mile east of Bisbee. An alert sentry spied automobiles running without their lights. The vehicles halted down the road, coinciding with the sentry's spying of someone dashing "out of the tent in which a number of machine guns had been stored, and make for the car." He pursued the fleeing man, who refused to halt when ordered to do so. With that, "[t]he sentry fired. The man pitched forward into the bottom of the car, dropping what was later found to be a machine gun. The car sped down the road followed by half dozen shots" unleashed by the sentry. Other troops responded and managed to stop "four unlighted cars, carrying eighteen men." They detained the occupants and escorted them to the city jail. Upon investigation, law enforcement concluded that "the story was much exaggerated. None of the eighteen Mexicans arrested near the scene of the attempted raid could be connected with the deed."

Another suspected smuggler, Dionsio Acosta, "was shot and seriously wounded just north of the international line by William Taylor, a private of the Ninth Cavalry, when he refused to halt at the sentry's command." Acosta continued to flee. "He staggered across the line and Mexicans helped him into Agua Prieta." As tensions mounted, Nellie Cowley predicted that a Huertista attack on Agua Prieta "would probably come from the east or south" but opined that "the bullets would come up this way." She also seemed secure in the knowledge of another artillery battery plus "two more regiments with orders to go across the line as soon as a shot falls on this side."

General Bliss arrived again at Naco, Arizona, to gather intelligence and access the possibility of the fight Nellie Crowley envisioned. In anticipation of Villa and Carranza's men striking against Maytorena and Gil's forces, the War Department ordered all officers and enlisted men to report to their commands, as well as "the renewal of army activities at the border forts and along the entire border" that indicated a shift in U.S. policy to take a staunch stand.

GOOD FEELINGS REMAIN

At this juncture, as indicated, both the Ninth and Tenth Cavalry regiments combined troops as the possibility of escalation loomed large. They influenced at least one local writer to observe "an exceptional comparison between military training and real military camps as conducted by the Ninth and Tenth cavalry companies camped just across the line from Naco." In contrast to the Mexican encampment across the border, where the garrison "left the entrails of steers lying on the ground…when they butchered in the streets prior to issuing rations" and where they allowed "their trash and swill to lie about," the American troops kept their site clean and neat and disposed of refuse in the earth dump pits they dug.

Black troops drew additional praise after they helped extinguish flames in Naco, Arizona. Some of them assisted residents. They recovered "furniture and other materials from the buildings in the path of the flames, but it was their efforts which cleared the fences and small sheds in the neighborhood of the fire from their reach and kept the sparks from setting fire to other structures." They battled the blaze with water buckets filled from a hydrant.

Other positive contributions included the Ninth Cavalry's payday, which "was accompanied by the usual increased activity in Naco and some increase of activity in this city," which happily was marked by "orderliness" admired by residents. Some townsmen concluded that "the conduct of the colored troopers was the best." Little wonder, then, that when speculation again arose that the Ninth Cavalry might withdraw from Douglas, albeit only briefly "from border to participate in maneuvers," a local resident, probably reflecting the opinion of others, "opposed this proposed move because of problems along the border." Accordingly, speculation "that the Ninth Cavalry will also be withdrawn from Douglas and sent to Monterey, California," without information "whether or not more troops" would arrive as replacements, raised community concerns. Late in the year, Brigadier General Bliss's inspection of Douglas, Naco and Fort Huachuca, as well as "several camps along the border," ended trepidations above transfers, at least for the time being.

Troop strength remained adequate for the needs as they existed in late 1914. This meant that the two troops of the Ninth Cavalry at Douglas and two troops of the Tenth Cavalry at Fort Huachuca were vital elements "of eighteen troops of cavalry, two machine gun platoons and three batteries of artillery." The concentration of forces did not halt casualties, which by

December totaled "five killed, forty-seven wounded and five struck by bullets and shells, but only scratched or bruised." To avoid or at least minimize further deaths and injuries, orders relocated the encampment of the Ninth and Tenth Cavalry "to afford better protection for men and horses."

DEFENSE MEASURES

The new locale stood back a mile from the border, as opposed to the previous position of only a quarter mile away from the international line. Besides the relative safety afforded by this site, troopers of the Ninth and Tenth enjoyed amenities such as piped water and good quarters. Bolstered by fifty more newly arrived troopers and the artillery from El Paso, encamped "alongside the camps of the Ninth and Tenth cavalry," the situation seemed well in hand. Indeed, the one troop of the Ninth Cavalry sent from Douglas and one troop of the Tenth Cavalry from Fort Huachuca, along with five hundred artillerymen, constituted a respectable garrison of approximately "of 2,500 men of the United States army on the border." Even so, their numbers approached only half the estimated strength of five thousand Mexicans in the combined Federalist commands of Gil and Maytorena.

Early in 1915, more changes emerged. Plans called for the entire Ninth Cavalry to depart from Naco, leaving only the first squadron of the Tenth Cavalry along the border, "the rest being ordered to Douglas and Fort Sill, Oklahoma." Predictably, "the Business Men's Protective Association, the Warren District Commercial Club, the mayor and other organizations and citizens" took action. Proponents of retaining the regiment wired Arizona's senators, requesting their intercession "with the secretary of war in keeping the troops at Naco for some time to come." Movement of the troops away from the district long had "been in the minds of the local people," some of whom realized that the proposed transfer came down to economic feasibility particularly water rates. Surmounting this hurdle and others took on paramount importance to convince authorities to retain the soldiers "based on the belief that the troops can do more good for the people of Cochise county stationed at Naco than they can in any other along the border."

For the time being, affairs in Mexico aided their cause. A falling out between Villa and Carranza spilled over elsewhere. That included Naco,

Arizona, which "had been subjected for weeks to a hail of 'stray bullets' from the Mexican lines during the siege" that finally ended in December 1914. A squadron of the Ninth Cavalry returned to its former post. Others followed as the War Department added more troops "along the border in Arizona and Texas due to raids of Mexican bandits," which also aided the cause of retaining the Tenth Cavalry in the region.

Commenting on the latest turn of events, Nellie Crowley mused, "It looks like the Mexican trouble was starting." She correctly ventured further: "If Wilson recognizes Carranza, he will have made a very foolish move, but it looks as if he would be going to. Then another revolution starts at once, probably headed by Villa." Little time passed before Villa achieved a principal part in the revolution, although his position was precarious. Crowley felt confident that the new commanding officer, Major General Fredrick Funston, would take the necessary actions.

She had cause to examine her claim after Villa appeared in Agua Prieta. Funston responded. At first, he moved the Black soldiers out of the trenches farther away from possible harm should Villa attack the enemy, "but moved them back about 8:00 o'clock" in the evening to prevent Villa's men from

The international border from Naco, Sonora, Mexico, looking into Naco, Arizona, photographed during the Mexican Revolution. A Buffalo Soldier stands guard by the border markers, the boundary between the two nations long before any barriers existed. One marker reads "92 B." *Courtesy the Bisbee Mining & Historical Museum, Fred Valenzuela Collection.*

The Ninth Cavalry's distinctive unit insignia, originally approved on October 22, 1925, featured a Native American arrayed in a breech cloth and war bonnet, mounted on a galloping pony, brandishing a rifle in his right and holding a single rein in his left hand, all in gold, displayed on a five-bastioned fort in blue edged with gold. The mounted warrior represented the regiment's frontier campaigns, while the five-bastioned fort was the badge of the Fifth Army Corps in Cuba, of which the Ninth Cavalry was a part. Yellow outlines in the design symbolize the cavalry. A blue fort represents active service in the Spanish-American War. The regimental motto proclaims, "We Can, We Will."
Courtesy the author.

"slipping over the American side to strike Agua Prieta from the north." For the moment, quiet settled over the area, as Cowley noted. With a perceived end to the threat, the Ninth Cavalry finally received marching orders. Cowley informed her mother that the regiment was slated for heading out on Christmas night. She added that "if there is no other trouble in Sonora, I suppose more troops will be taken away." Subsequent events countered her forecast. Not long after she thought peace had been achieved, tens of thousands of American troops would pour into the borderlands.

Previously, during the late summer of 1915, the Ninth Cavalry had learned of its assignment in the Philippines. Now it responded to its latest orders. Perhaps another letter from Nellie Suydam Cowley, sent in December 1915, best captured the regiment's final departure from Arizona. She recorded, "The Seventh cavalry got here a day ago and today the Ninth leave. They stepped off down Ninth street on foot with their guns, knapsacks, overcoats, in fact, in full marching order."

By December 29, the Ninth Cavalry, "one of the best regiments in the service, and which recently received high praise from the Secretary of War for the way in which it has done patrol work on the Mexican border," had reached the Presidio of San Francisco. The unit remained there until January 5, when its tested veterans sailed again, this time for Manila.

With the Ninth Cavalry's departure for the Philippines, the regiment left behind a credible record. On many levels, the regiment's sojourn in Arizona embodied the roles played by its brother regiments at one time or another in Arizona. Indeed, the unit performed a variety of functions carried on later by other agencies of the U.S. government. Most significantly, the Ninth's personnel acted in a credible, professional manner. Despite a few events of lawless behavior, racial hostilities associated with the posting of Black troops to the Arizona/Sonora borderlands tended to be minimal. The relative good will that remained as the cavalrymen were transferred across the Pacific was commendable. Despite their contributions, volatile events in Mexico remained a challenge to be faced by their brother Buffalo Soldiers, who continued to serve in Arizona well into the twentieth century.

Chapter 2

Tenth Cavalry

"Ready and Forward"

ORIGINS

The same 1866 Congressional act that brought about the formation of the Ninth Cavalry in Louisiana likewise provided for its brother regiment, the Tenth Cavalry. This unit assembled in Kansas. At first, the officers and men slowly gathered at Fort Leavenworth. After that, the Tenth relocated to Fort Riley. Eventually, the regiment moved to Indian Territory (Oklahoma) and Texas. The latter locale remained its main area of operation until, after nearly two decades, the War Department transferred the entire unit, which heretofore had been scattered at several forts in the Lone Star State. Principally deployed against Kiowa and Comanche stalwarts as well as other missions along the border with Mexico, the troops now would be sent as part of the major strike force against the Apaches. Rumors in 1885 about their major move from Texas westward proved true.

MARCH TO ARIZONA

During that spring, as John Glass's regimental history indicated, after spending decades in Texas, the Tenth U.S. Cavalry made its way to "the Department of Arizona, marching along the Southern Pacific Railroad." As the column took up its march from Fort Davis, it comprised eleven troops

When the photographer took this picture at Fort Apache during March 1887, men of Troop A, Tenth U.S. Cavalry, had settled into Arizona after years of service in Texas. *Courtesy University of Arizona Library Special Collections.*

Duty in the desert sometimes necessitated transporting water when leaving for an extended period from the fort. Patrols dispatched from Troop I of the Tenth Cavalry were no exception. *Courtesy Library of Congress.*

In 1886, Troop I, Tenth Cavalry, arrived at Fort Verde. The men turned out on the parade ground astride their well-groomed mounts. *Courtesy Library of Congress.*

and the band. At Camp Rice, Troop I joined the entourage. From that point to Bowie Station, Arizona, the twelve troops continued together in a rare reunion because the regiment had not been together since its establishment in 1866. Then, the short-lived gathering ended at Bowie, where "the troops separated to go to their several stations."

Regimental headquarters under its first and long-serving colonel, Benjamin H. Grierson, a Civil War veteran best known for his raid deep into the South, arrived at Fort Whipple outside Prescott. With Grierson and his

headquarters contingent came both the talented Tenth Cavalry band and Troop B, the three elements totaling about ninety-two noncommissioned officers, troopers and bandsmen. The other units of the Tenth fanned out to Fort Apache (Troop A), Fort Thomas (Troops C, F and G), Fort Grant (Troops D, E, H, K and L) and Fort Verde (Troops I and M). Later, the band, Troop B and headquarters relocated to a series of other garrisons, while elements of the regiment also rotated to and from the San Carlos Apache Reservation.

Even in garrison, water was not always easily obtained. At Fort Verde, a wagon driven by a Tenth Cavalry enlisted man hauled a regular water supply from the nearby Verde River. *Courtesy Library of Congress.*

VIEWS FROM THE TERRITORIAL PRESS

Even before the regiment set foot into Arizona, the regional press often leveled negative comments against the army in the territory, whether white or Black. For one example, the Tucson *Arizona Weekly Citizen* decried the lack of result to end the Apache campaign. The editorial challenged the commanding general, George Crook, "to publish a list of the killed and wounded soldiers and officers in the recent Indian campaign. Even the squaws and papooses evaded the argus-eyed military and reached Mexico in safety by the most practicable route."

Once in the territory, the regiment incurred more lampooning. For instance, only a month after arriving, four companies of the Tenth offered another soapbox for anti-Crook sentiments. The June 17, 1885 *Clifton Clarion* ran an op-ed with the headline "A March without a Result." The writer did not blame this "body of troops," who made "quite an extended march, per orders from Gen. Crook, through Arizona and New Mexico." The fault was for "not having accomplished something during the campaign" because constrained rules of engagement hampered "them to a certain line of action." The reporter noted, however, that the officers felt a "certain sense humiliated from the fact of having effected nothing. Yet they have no grounds to feel so, as they have had no chance, as others have had, to show whether they were equal to any occasion that might have arisen in bringing the Indians to an engagement."

He advocated that while "[t]he officers or the colored soldiers have had no show," they should not be categorized with former unsuccessful military commands "until they are tried." The correspondent could have added another challenge faced by being dispatched to the field so soon after taking station in Arizona. As another newspaper indicated, "The horses belonging to the regiment are reported to be badly used up by the trip from Texas as to prevent longer marches than eight or ten Miles a day." Decidedly, in operations against a highly mobile, swift-moving enemy, that pace was inadequate.

Either ignorant or indifferent to this debilitating factor, the *Deming Tribune* caustically concluded, "The colored troop of the Tenth cavalry have left the Territory for Camp Grant, Arizona. They fought nobody." The oft-antagonistic *Daily Tombstone Epitaph* later added its own racist, facetious jab: "There is no truth in the report that Crook, Zulick and Geronimo intend to go into the circus business, with a minstrel and base ball troupe from the Tenth Cavalry as the leading attraction."

Balking at negative references, especially about the misconduct of the men "in the towns along their line of march" to their various posts, some of the regiment's officers became "indignant at the reports of the papers," or so Clifton's *Clarion* for May 6, 1885, announced. In truth, when elements of the regiment proceeded to their prescribed assignments, they halted along the route. The *Clarion* admitted that the troops "conducted themselves in a becoming manner."

After the various elements of the Tenth dispersed to their new assignments, opportunities arose to prove or disprove the mixed pre-publicity they had received. This particularly was true at one of the few posts manned by the African American cavalrymen adjacent to a civilian community. Once regimental headquarters and Troop B reported to Fort Whipple on Prescott's outskirts, locals could form their own views about their new military neighbors.

At that point, Prescott's *Miner* partially recanted its original pejorative stance. On May 15, 1885, the paper admitted that "the unenviable reputation given the Tenth Cavalry by certain journals in Southern New Mexico and Arizona" was unfounded. Further, these cavalrymen showed "no disposition to rival the legendary 'Bloody Fourteenth'" Infantry, a unit manned by white soldiers who previously garrisoned nearby Fort Whipple. Instead, the troopers of the Tenth Cavalry were "well behaved and as soldierly looking set of men that have ever been stationed at Whipple."

Despite an apparent reversal in editorial point of view, elsewhere in the same edition, while the paper complimented incoming Troop B as one of the best-drilled cavalry companies "in Uncle Sam's service," a reporter could not refrain from marring his positive perspective by tagging on a bigoted epithet when he referred to the horse soldiers as "Dandy Coons." In contrast, news of the pending arrival of Black troopers so impressed one of Prescott's only African American residents that he supposedly vowed that "as soon as the 'colored sojers' arrived he was 'qwine to jine de army.'"

Perhaps the town's saloonkeepers were not as awed with the Black soldiers. The reason for this possible disappointment among the community's bar owners was based on a contention that the men of the Tenth spent "less money on ardent spirits than any other troops stationed at Whipple." Instead, allegedly, "Their special weakness" was "swell clothing in the ultra dude design." Given the fact that most of the soldiers previously had served in relative isolation in Texas for a long period, easy access to fashionable civilian attire for off-duty wear probably was a welcome luxury.

An additional motivation for acquiring this new sartorial splendor may have stemmed from a desire to please the wives, daughters, laundresses and others of the fairer sex who would be joining the cavalrymen at their new assignments in Arizona. Among these were four ladies who came to town in advance of the troopers on a May 14 stagecoach: Mrs. George Washington Lafayette Johnson, Mrs. John Quincy Adams Jefferson, Mrs. Patrick Henry Andrew Jackson and Mrs. George Trumbull Buchanan.

STRIKE UP THE BAND

It is more than likely that these ladies were married to noncommissioned officers who earned a slightly higher pay and thereby could afford being married. This possibly was the case for Mrs. George Washington Lafayette Johnson, whose spouse was probably Corporal George Johnson of the regimental band, which "Papers of Southern Arizona" praised for its talent.

Indeed, these martial bandsmen had developed an impressive library of musical scores and gained a reputation for excellence in great part because the Tenth Cavalry's colonel in early life had been a music teacher. Prescottonians quickly could judge the quality of these bandsmen from personal experience.

Just over a week after the Tenth Cavalry came to the territorial capital, the bandsmen received an invitation to lead the Decoration Day (now known as Memorial Day) observances. Further, Troop B's commanding officer, Captain Robert Geno Smither, presided as grand marshal. It was the band, however, that headed the procession. After the ceremonies in the Courthouse Plaza, the musicians returned to the fort in a wagon. Unfortunately, a wheel broke along the way, injuring some of them—"one so severely as to cause a doubt to whether he would recover or not."

This mishap did not deter continued interest in the military musicians. One of the community's two militia companies lost little time in securing the group to perform for their benefit. In early June, residents were informed of "the Promenade Concert given by the 10th Cavalry Band, under the auspices of the Prescott Rifles, at the new City Hall." Tickets were available for gentlemen and ladies at two dollars. Such popular performances prompted the *Miner* to exhort, "The excellent band of the Tenth Cavalry would confer a favor on the citizens of Prescott by following the example of the musicians of the Third [Cavalry] by giving a weekly concert in the Court House Plaza."

It is not clear from existing sources whether this suggestion was acted on, although near the end of its stay at Fort Whipple, the band evidently did play for Troop B before the troopers departed for San Carlos in May 1886. To commemorate this event, "The colored soldiers gave a farewell dance at Whipple last evening prior to taking their departure today." Moreover, as part of this farewell, the regimental adjutant, Lieutenant Samuel Woodward, "had the 10th Cavalry band out today for mounted drill with their instruments and favored our town with a general serenade. The entire band was mounted on white steeds and presented a fine appearance, while they discoursed sweet strains of music." Once again, later in the month, the musicians of the Tenth did the honors at Decoration Day observances for 1886, much as they had the prior year, all led by English-born chief musician Charles Goldsbury, who had risen to head the regimental band nearly three years after his enlistment in the Tenth Cavalry on May 3, 1883.

As would occur in a later era, when the Ninth Cavalry patrolled along the border with Mexico, baseball games sometimes pitted civilian teams against troops from Fort Whipple. These friendly matchups helped break down racial barriers. In at least one instance, after the Tenth Cavalry's headquarters transferred to Fort Grant, the *Daily Tombstone* recording a duel for the championship of Arizona Territory "between a nine from the 4th Cavalry, stationed at Ft. Huachuca, and one from the 10th Cavalry, stationed at Ft. Grant." In what was a high-scoring game, the playoff "resulted in a victory for the Huachuca nine by a score of 21 to 11." Generations later, military teams from other regiments often played the Tenth Cavalry, as did an array of civilian teams from Bisbee, Douglas, Nogales and elsewhere in the state.

GARRISON LIFE

The men of the Tenth Cavalry participated in more than slugfests on the diamond. In fact, for the most part at all their duty stations, they found themselves assigned to the many monotonous tasks of garrison life. Typically, this meant cleaning building interiors and grounds. Further, they occasionally constructed or repaired existing edifices or assisted civilian contractors. These chores might entail improvements of the quality of their lives, such as the completion of an icehouse and waterworks at Fort Thomas. Then there were a range of other responsibilities, from kitchen police to inspections, target practice and guard duty.

Both at the fort and in the field, bugle calls punctuated each phase from sunrise to beyond sunset. On one of his excursions to the West, up-and-coming artist Frederic Remington found a bugle at Fort Grant caught his

Hunting excursions from Fort Verde afforded officers and a fortunate few Tenth Cavalry troopers the opportunity to leave the daily post routine behind, as well as provided fresh game to supplement their rather monotonous daily government diet. *Courtesy Library of Congress.*

Troop K, 10th Cavalry at volley-firing. Fort Thomas, Ariz.

At Fort Thomas, Troop K, Tenth Cavalry, under the watchful eyes of Lieutenant Powhattan Clarke, engaged in target practice to hone their marksmanship skills. *Courtesy the author.*

attention playing "some very inspiring call." A brother of one of Remington's publishers, First Lieutenant John Bigelow, added more details. He noted that while assigned in the mid-1880s to a southern Arizona outpost, his captain established the calls that accompanied a representative regimen.

During the late 1880s, Forrestine Cooper, eldest daughter of a troop commander in the Tenth, shared similar recollections from the viewpoint of a young girl growing up on an army post. Her memories from Fort Grant recalled "the time of day we children knew by the bugle calls." She went on to muse, "From the cannon salute at sunrise, when the flag was raised to the top of the flagstaff that stood in the center of the parade ground, until the sound of taps, the signal for lights out in the barracks, the daily home routine was planned according to official duties of the officers. We children were told to 'come home at the first call for stables,' or retreat call, water call, guard-mounting, dinner call, fatigue call, tattoo. The hour of day or night meant nothing to us as a period of time. Bugle calls measured the hours of officers, soldiers, women, and children in garrison life."

In the early 1890s, at Fort Huachuca, a typical day began with reveille at 5:45 a.m. After dressing and heading to the mess hall for the morning meal, fatigue duties started at 7:30 a.m., followed by recall at 12:15 p.m. With the conclusion of dinner, the men resumed fatigue duties or attended schools or other training. At 4:30 p.m., once more recall rang out that ended afternoon tasks, followed at 4:45 p.m. to 5:15 p.m. by drill. A guard mount assembled at 5:30 p.m. Military requirements ended, freeing the troops not on evening duty to eat supper. Tattoo echoed at 9:00 p.m. and was followed by taps.

Bugle calls thus embodied the prescribed rounds that made up the life of officers and men in Arizona "occupied in work, details, drills, garrison courts…boards of survey" and a list of the of time-consuming "week-long sameness of the days" only "broken by the pomp of full-dress inspection on Sunday." It was on that day and "after the morning inspection officers and troopers had the rest of the day off," or so wrote Second Lieutenant Powhattan Clarke, the junior subaltern of Troop K, Tenth Cavalry, from Fort Grant.

CAMP AT BONITA CAÑON

While some enjoyed the relative comforts of Fort Grant, which even boasted a manmade water feature where officers and their families could canoe, another young member of the Tenth Cavalry spent a more rustic brief experience at a semipermanent field encampment. Teenager Forrestine Cooper's father commanded Troop H, Tenth Cavalry. Captain Charles Lawrence Cooper's troop reported to one of many scattered outposts established by Brigadier General Crook. He dispatched the Tenth Cavalry and other units to key trails and waterholes in southern Arizona. Crook sought to deny Geronimo and other free-roaming Apaches access to water and key routes north from Mexico. He thought that he could hold the enemy in Sonora and eventually bring about their surrender.

Cooper's command was sent to Bonita Cañon on the west side of the Chiricahua Mountain Range. Troop H joined an earlier contingent dispatched to the site, Troop E, under Captain Joseph Kelly and later replaced the other detachment. Cooper's force performed ordinary camp, which meant, as Martin Tagg summarized in an archaeological report for the National Park Service, they "assumed the previous duties of the detachment, which at this time consisted primarily of carrying the mail, mounting an occasional patrol and escort, and, of course, guarding the waterhole." Months later, Troop E rejoined them. Ultimately, both Cooper and Kelley would depart when they returned to their garrison with the arrival of Troop I from Camp Verde.

After the assassination of President James A. Garfield, a Tenth Cavalry detail that served at Bonita Cañon erected a stone monument to the fallen commander-in-chief. Later, the stones served as the building materials for the fireplace at the Faraway Ranch's main house. *Courtesy National Park Service.*

Cooper's daughter Forrestine left a memoir that served as the basis for a later novel, *When Geronimo Rode*. She recalled arriving with her mother at this canyon, with its "high, rugged walls so close together as barely to allow space for the cavalry camp and a roadway past the brown-white tents nestled among live oak trees. Near the tents a stable had been constructed of logs and brush, and facing toward the end of the canyon it afforded protection for the horses during bad weather."

While the men lived under canvas in two-man "dog tents," the Coopers took up residence in a primitive cabin that stood on the site of latter-day Faraway Ranch house. Modifications furnished some amenities, while the family enjoyed a cook-housekeeper, Jenny Miller, the spouse of Sergeant Girard Miller, one of scores of Black enlisted men who spent time at Bonita Cañon. The presence of many of them remains evident in a rock memorial they created in their spare time dedicated to the memory of President Grover Cleveland. Several of them inscribed their names in the rocks as a unique reminder of their duty at this remote station, which otherwise would have been forgotten.

Following Sergeant Pollard Cole's retirement, he sent a photograph of his newborn son to Charles Faulkner, a former Tenth Cavalry "bunkie" with whom he served at Bonita Cañon. It was common for soldiers to form lasting friendships with their comrades given the close-knit nature and typically long-term service of Black army personnel on the frontier. *Courtesy the author.*

SCOUT WITH THE BUFFALO SOLDIERS

In a late 1960s interview, "Willie" Corbusier, the youngest son of Fort Grant's surgeon, fondly remembered the name of one of his family favorites. After engaging several unsuccessful household servants, the Corbusier family "at last secured [Henry] Jackson of the Hospital Corps as a striker." After the Black trooper enlisted, he reported to the Tenth Cavalry. In due course, Fort Grant's surgeon, Dr. William Corbusier, arranged for the private's reassignment to the hospital corps. Frederic Remington pressed Jackson, who had not yet transferred from the cavalry, into service as one of his models for his 1888 article, "A Scout with the Buffalo Soldiers." Supposedly, the Corbusier brood thought that Jackson "was just about perfection. It was 'Jackson this and Jackson that' on just about any subject and soon he was accepted as a very necessary part of our outfit."

A STUDY OF ACTION.

During the artist's stay at Fort Grant, Frederic Remington posed Dr. Willam Corbusier's "striker," Private Henry Jackson of the Tenth Cavalry, as one of his models for a *Harper's* article, published as "A Scout with the Buffalo Soldiers."

If they signed on to serve as an officer's "striker"—a man who provided a variety of services for room, board and extra money—enlisted men could add to their meager pay as well as escape living in barracks, plus they could even wed. The woman in the apron standing next to the private may be his spouse. *Courtesy Library of Congress.*

Dr. and Mrs. William Corbusier's family included five sons, one of whom recalled Frederic Remington's stay at Fort Grant, Arizona, while gathering information for his 1888 *Harper's Weekly* article about the Buffalo Soldiers. *Courtesy the author.*

Jackson was but one of the subjects Remington observed during his 1888 outing to Fort Grant and its environs. While there, in a pithy musing, Remington displayed racism tempered by his genuine admiration for the Black troopers: "These nigs are the best d[amned] soldiers in the world." The artist-reporter further noted that the only reply ever heard from them when they received an order was "Yes sir," without further comment or complaint.

Troop K's First Sergeant William Givens markedly impressed Remington. This able, dependable, long-service soldier earned a respect that helped the Tenth gain an enviable reputation. Many other contemporaries of Givens's likewise deserved recognition. What appears to be examples of such men were a pair of troopers whom the local Prescott press mentioned as receiving leave, which constituted a mark of trust. Sergeant L.M. Smith of Troop E, Tenth Cavalry, was granted a furlough for two months with the proviso that this excused absence take "effect after his re-enlistment." Another cavalryman, Sergeant Joseph Jenkins from Troop A at Fort Apache, likewise gained a two-month furlough. No doubt in both instances, they demonstrated reliability to return and rejoin their unit afterward to fulfill their reenlistment commitments.

VIOLENCE AND MUTINY

In contrast, a few individuals sometimes marred the sterling status of the Tenth Cavalry. Courts-martial among the troops were not uncommon for Black and white soldiers alike. While often the latter group regularly received courts-martial because of desertion, African American troops tended to remain for the full span of their enlistment and often reenlisted as well. Of course, exceptions existed.

An unusual outbreak occurred in 1887. At an encampment of the Tenth Cavalry, a patrol halted in Mogollon Mountains; after being summoned back to Fort Verde, their commander, Captain John Baldwin, left his patrol. Dr. Edgar Mearns, the medico at their post, remained as the only commissioned officer with the contingent. Their supplies soon ran low, a circumstance that prompted a potential mutiny. In desperation, the troopers mounted their horses, intent on leaving the bivouac. Before they could ride away, Mearns returned from a neighboring store with food he had purchased. Distributing the rations, he then convinced the men to remain in camp. Nevertheless, four ringleaders ended in irons and stood court-martial. During the hearing, several of their comrades appeared as witnesses. The doctor also testified for the defense.

In contrast, one more atypical illustration stood out among the few others that occurred in Arizona. Soon after the disappearance of a Tenth Cavalry bandsman, a telegram was dispatched. In this instance, the terse language to the city marshal of Phoenix read, "William Russell, mulatto, medium height, scar on nose deserted from this post on 9th. May be with circus which recently left here. Thirty dollars reward if delivered to post." Ultimately, the would-be new circus performer was apprehended, and a reward was paid by the military for his return to stand trial. Those convicted of serious military infractions, including desertion, went under guard to Kansas to serve their sentences at Fort Leavenworth military prison or were sent to Alcatraz. This was the fate of Robert L. Burton, Marlin W. Beahl and Joseph Seon, all former privates with the Tenth Cavalry pronounced military convicts in 1889.

Another "colored soldier, belonging to the tenth cavalry," sought a different means of prematurely ending his stint with the regiment. He attempted suicide at the Fort Whipple's corral. The distraught man shot "himself through the head with a carbine." Although the unnamed trooper lost a portion of his nose, "he did not inflict serious injury."

That was not so for another attempted suicide, which ended in not one death but two. As recorded by the *Miner* on December 14, 1887, "Among the cases recently placed on the court docket here was a divorce case entitled, Dandridge vs Dandridge. The case has, however, been taken to a higher court, by the murder, recently, of Jane Dandridge, one of the parties to the suit, by her paramour, Alfred J. Moss, Troop A, 10th Cavalry, at Fort Apache. After killing Mrs. Dandridge, Moss committed suicide." Evidently, "Moss became exceedingly jealous of the woman, so much so, that, as he says in a letter written and left by him, 'he could stand it no longer,' and determined to put an end to his and her existence," according to the St. Johns, Arizona *Herald* of December 8, 1887.

In 1888, a second homicide took place, this time at Fort Grant. The victim, Troop E trumpeter James Cox, died at the hands of "Robert Campbell, a private in the same troop." The alleged motive was that Cox failed to pay Campbell five dollars that the "latter owed him." A summary in the October 6, 1888 *Arizona Weekly Citizen* noted that "hot words passed between the two. Cox finally threatened to slap Campbell's face, and the latter told him if he said he would kill him. Upon Cox carrying his threat into execution, Campbell, drew a pistol and shot him dead. Campbell was turned over to the United States civil authorities."

More complex, convoluted causes left Troop E, Tenth Cavalry's Private William Fleming dead at San Carlos. Sergeant James Logan, suspected of leading a gang that murdered Fleming, went to jail with others who may have played a hand in the lethal plot. Logan purportedly feared court-martial after the presumed perpetrator and victim quarreled. Afterward, on about July 20, 1889, Logan threatened Fleming, telling the private that "he had better desert or he would regret it. At that time, the sergeant stated that if Fleming did go, he [Logan] would give him the advantage of five day's start by not reporting him absent."

Logan punctuated his demands: "You can be in hell by that time," followed by "a string of abusive epithets," in the words of a Phoenix, Arizona *Republican* article.

Despite belief by law enforcement that Logan killed Fleming, others likewise were taken into custody. A grand jury jointly indicted a trio consisting of Jefferson Wilson, David Edwards and Primas Douglass. The first named defendant demanded a severance from the other two men.

Moreover, one more name appeared to complicate the issue. At first, Private William Varnum was arrested. While incarcerated, he made a preposterous declaration. Varnum's version of the tragedy involved "an organization in E troop, similar to the Mollie Maguires or Ku Klux," or so the soldier insisted. For a time, he refused to give all the plotters' names, but he did implicate Douglass, Wilson and Edwards as members of the secret society charged with Fleming's slaying. Furthermore, Varnum confessed that he decoyed Fleming from the fort.

In May 1890, Private Varnum took the stand. There he told a different tale. He had previously signed a statement that he had witnessed the decoying of Fleming and that the victim had his head smashed with an iron bar. Now he denied all knowledge of the murder. The prosecution successfully challenged Varnum's contrary account in court. It relied heavily on his past sworn deposition to bolster their case. They also strengthened the prosecution by introducing a bloodstained gray flannel shirt that had been discovered days after Fleming's death and which belonged to Wilson.

Despite a determined defense, the May 30, 1890 *Arizona Republican* opened with the headline, "Wilson Convicted of Flemings Murder. He Takes the Result Very Bravely. The Jury Deliberated for Six Hours Before They Were Able to Agree on a Verdict." Jefferson Wilson, late private in Troop K, Tenth Cavalry, was the first to face his fate. Meanwhile, Edwards, Douglass, Logan and Varnum still awaited their day in court.

Undaunted, Wilson's attorneys attempted to save their client based on a legal technicality. They went so far as to prepare a petition to the U.S. Supreme Court at Washington asking release of Jefferson Wilson. They claimed that Wilson's indictment by a fifteen-member Maricopa County grand jury under an 1887 Arizona Territory code ran contrary to the later statute of the Fifteenth Legislature requiring from seventeen to twenty-three to men for this purpose. The Supreme Court rejected the appeal. The chief justice wrote that the "legality or illegality of the Grand Jury cannot be raised collaterally, provided twelve jurors concurred in finding the indictment."

Wilson indeed temporarily escaped capital punishment because of a technicality when he faced a retrial at another venue because one of his former attorneys now served on the bench where the hearing was to take place. Once again, the *Arizona Republican* followed the saga in the June 17, 1893 issue. It noted that after languishing in Maricopa County for the past three years, he left Florence, the initial site of his second trial, "that being now in the district in which the crime is alleged to have been committed," for Tucson. Without funds to engage a defense, the county's undersheriff, A. Barry, provided money to hire legal representation! Tucson's *Arizona Weekly Citizen*, also published on June 17, 1893, offered an explanation for this extraordinary support. In Phoenix, Wilson had "been their 'good boy' in the jail. He has behaved himself perfectly. At one time when other prisoners were escaping he gave the alarm." In fact, jailers regarded him as a model prisoner.

One week later, the *Arizona Weekly Citizen* ran another revealing article: "Jeff Wilson, the prisoner released yesterday after being in custody four years, left last night for Phoenix, where he made many friends, to look for employment." While he could still be indicted, the prosecution's key witnesses had scattered. The post surgeon went to England. No one knew how to contact him. Varnum, the mercurial player in this strange drama, added to this narrative of "ill luck, disaster, and death of the other three men who were acquitted of the crime." According to the sometimes fanciful former private, Logan died of a gunshot received in North Dakota. Varnum likewise claimed that on his deathbed, Logan confessed that he had murdered Fleming. The third man, Douglass, went back to his troop after being released. At San Carlos, he was thrown from his mount. The resulting injuries claimed his life.

The fourth person of interest, David Edwards, broke his legs in a railway accident. As recounted in the May 18, 1893 *Arizona Republican*, "death soon followed." As a sort of epilogue, the reporter concluded, "According to

Varnum's information, these casualties occurred almost simultaneously so that those who believe in a providential influence in earthly affairs take the violent death of these men to be an evidence of their guilt."

Regardless of Varnum's veracity or possible fabrication, Wilson escaped the gallows. Soon after his arrival in Phoenix, he operated a small store near the railroad depot, which he ran with a business partner, José Apadaca. In early January 1894, a pair of thieves staged a break-in and stole the cash. The sheriff's office soon rounded up two persons of interest. Among the evidence against them was a concealed pittance of $3.60 in nickels and dimes.

Nearly eight months later, another burglar struck. This time the target was a store owned by R. Wilson (no relation). Previously, a thief or thieves made off with a hefty $500 or so from Wilson's establishment. The next attempt ended with a dead burglar whom the night watchman killed with a shotgun. The slain man was approximately thirty-five years old, unmarried and without known relatives in the Phoenix area. The local police and justice's courts knew him from his past criminal escapes. He was none other than José Apadaca. Earlier in the year, Wilson and perhaps Apadaca closed their Monroe Street retail operation, which had failed.

Varnum, also known as William Varnon and Henry Varnom, likewise took up life in Phoenix after leaving the army as a free man. The imaginative raconteur obtained a position as a porter in a local hotel. Despite territorial laws prohibiting such a union, he married a white woman "of the Mormon faith." Eventually, they relocated to Tucson, where he sought new employment. The couple's days there allowed them to set aside sufficient money from his $8 per week plus board working for Henrietta Herring Franklin, the spouse of Selim M. Franklin, at their stately brick Main Street residence. The Varnums managed to raise three children and acquire a half lot for $100, where they built their own home. Others implicated in murder did not share this fortunate end.

MURDER MOST FOUL

Take the case of Frank Nelson, a discharged Black soldier who murdered Sarah McHarris and her three-year-old child. As the *St. Johns Herald* for August 7, 1890, speculated, he presumably acted "through jealousy." McHarris, the reporter added, was "the husband of the unfortunate woman" and served as "a soldier belonging to troop H, Tenth cavalry, now stationed at Fort

Apache." After being arrested, Nelson went to trial, where his attorney made "a strong plea to the court for mercy but to no avail and the court sentenced him to hang on the 19th day of December." Two days before his scheduled execution, his first of five stays of execution kept Nelson from the gallows until June 1891. The petition for the commutation of sentence to life imprisonment based on good behavior while jailed failed.

Pennsylvania native Frank Nelson, former member of Company C, Twenty-Fourth Infantry, in which he served for a decade, received baptism from a Roman Catholic priest. Later that afternoon, at three o'clock on July 3, 1891, as the *Arizona Republican* summarized, Nelson in his final moments "ascended the scaffold without hesitation…then repeated the Lord's prayer, arose from his knees with tears in his eyes." Then the sheriff sprang the trap. The physician waited for approximately three minutes before he pronounced Nelson dead. Nonetheless, he ordered that Nelson remain hanging for twelve more minutes.

TRAILING GERONIMO

More commonly, however, Black cavalrymen faced death or injury from another source: the Apaches who sought to live free of restrictive reservations. Almost immediately upon taking up their new posts in Arizona, commanders sent four companies from Fort Grant into the field to join the campaign against the master of guerrilla tactics, Geronimo. For months, elements of the Tenth roamed the Sierra Madres in pursuit of him and his small band of determined followers. Some forays resulted in close combat. For example, from April through May 1886, Captain Thomas C. Lebo, in command of Troop K, Tenth Cavalry, set out on a two-hundred-mile chase against the highly mobile opponent. Early in the month, he closed with the elusive enemy. On May 3, according to one contemporary account, "The Indians held their ground and made an attempt to get" the troopers' mounts, but these efforts were "frustrated by a covering force and a detail sent to drive the herd to the rear. Each side in the fight numbered about thirty men. Three Indians were seen to fall and to be dragged back out of fire, a pretty sure indication that they were killed or mortally wounded."

As the fight raged, men of Troop K also sustained casualties. A Tenth cavalryman was killed, while another Black soldier, Corporal Edward Scott, was "disabled with a serious wound, exposed to the enemy's fire."

The circa 1880s caption on this photograph reads, "Corporal Edward Scott, 10th U.S. Cavalry. Shot by Apaches at Sierra Pinito, Mexico, May 3rd, 1885. Thigh amputated May 8th, 1886. Operator: Paul R. Brown, M.D." *Courtesy Otis Historical Archives, National Museum of Health and Medicine, CP 1855, OHA 75 Contributed Photographs Collection.*

Disregarding his own life, Captain Lebo's second in command, Lieutenant Powhattan Clarke, braved murderous sniping to rush Corporal Edward Scott, who "lay disabled with a serious wound, exposed to the enemy's fire." The wounded corporal survived but eventually had to have a leg amputated, but not before a grueling ride back to Fort Huachuca's hospital, all the while making the trip "without a groan."

This action above the call of duty earned the young West Point graduate a Medal of Honor and a degree of fame. His enhanced visibility stemmed largely from a comradeship that developed between Clarke and an up-and-coming eastern artist, Frederic Remington.

After this encounter with the detail from Troop K, Lebo and Clarke rode into Nogales, Arizona, at daylight. On May 4, 1886, the mounts and men had barely rested when they were reinforced by Troop B of the Fourth U.S. Cavalry and were back in the saddle, leaving at 1:00 a.m. for a "second attack which it is proposed to make on the Apaches" near the site of the May 3 engagement. By May 9, Lebo and his forty-two men were "in a position to ambush the Indians on the south side of the Cananeas [Mountains], in which direction" Troop K drove the enemy toward another two troops of U.S. Cavalry.

This would not be Clarke's last close encounter with indomitable Apache warriors. A few years later, he joined a task force in pursuit of the outlaw

Indian scouts and handpicked troopers from the Tenth Cavalry formed a formidable strike force, led by Lieutenant Clarke. During the 1880s and early 1890s, they pursued Geronimo and other Apaches resisting reservation life. *Courtesy Freeman's-Hindman Auctions.*

Indian scout the Apache Kid and a handful of other holdouts who avoided captivity after Geronimo had been forcibly removed from the territory in 1886. Along with another white officer, a sergeant, an African American cavalrymen and Native American scouts, Clarke once more engaged in a duel that could have cost him his life. He survived, while three others in the patrol, including a Yavapai scout known as "Rowdy" and a Black Tenth Cavalry trooper named William McBryar, earned their Medals of Honor. Born in North Carolina, the five-foot, five-and-a-half-inch McBryar rose from private to first sergeant in Troop K. On March 7, 1890, he distinguished himself "for coolness, bravery, and good marksmanship against Apaches at Salt River," according to an account that quickly worked its way up the chain of command in recognition of his valor.

NEW HORIZONS

This action occurred near the end of the Tenth's tenure in Arizona. Colonel John K. Mizner wrote to the U.S. Army's adjutant general requesting a reassignment of his regiment. He stressed that the Tenth had been stationed south of the thirty-sixth latitude for more than two decades. He contended, with some slight exaggeration, that no other cavalry regiment had "been subject to so great an amount of hard, fatigueing [*sic*] and continueing" [*sic*] service as the Tenth." For their exemplary performance, Mizner claimed that his men deserved to be sent "to as good stations as can be assigned." He specifically requested a gradual change of climate, with assignment no farther north than Kansas, the first duty station where the unit had formed in the 1860s. His superiors obliged. From the several dispersed permanent posts and field camps, such as the one in Bonito Cañon, the regiment packed and proceeded during midwinter from Arizona's sunny clime for the icy tundra of Montana.

By 1898, the Tenth Cavalry, along with the other three regiments manned by Black enlisted men, had gained further laurels. After being dispatched to Cuba as part of the invasion force sent there during the short-lived Spanish-American War, they received considerable national attention. These heroes of San Juan Hill returned to the United States and headed to Texas, but only briefly. After the brisk battles in Cuba, they sailed to the island again, this time as law enforcement for the joint military and civilian government established by the United States in support of the transition from Spanish rule to emergence as an independent democratic nation—or so the theory ran.

While there, the Tenth chiefly performed periodic patrols, which in one instance resulted in an exchange between bandits and cavalrymen from Troop K. Generally, however, Cuba proved a quiet respite where several men found their treatment more congenial than in the United States. In fact, some of them married Cuban brides. Near the conclusion of 1899, the regiment sufficiently fulfilled its mission to the degree that the second squadron could make its way back to Texas and thence on the Philippines, while the first squadron remained in Cuba until it eventually departed as well, in its case to Fort Robinson, Nebraska.

HENRY O. FLIPPER

Simultaneous to the Tenth Cavalry's arrival in Arizona, and sometime after its departure, one of the regiment's former members entered and remained in the territory. Henry O. Flipper, the first African American graduate of the U.S. Military Academy, came to Arizona and engaged in a number of civilian occupations. Previously, after being assigned to the Tenth upon his graduation from West Point, he ran afoul of army regulations and at least one of his superiors. A subsequent court-martial found him guilty of "conduct unbecoming an officer." This verdict resulted in his dismissal from the army. For much of the remainder of his life, he unsuccessfully attempted to overturn the ruling. Likewise, over the ensuing decades, he attained a significant reputation in the borderlands, especially in Arizona. On June 5, 1895, the *Arizona Republic* reprinted a story from the Nogales *Vidette* that recognized Flipper as "a most competent civil engineer and surveyor." A few years later, the *Border Vidette* for April 15, 1899, praised Flipper as "one of the best authorities on land and mining laws of the United States and Mexico."

In fact, when he took up residence in that community, during October 1885, he remained a familiar figure for years to come. Several newspaper accounts continued to trace the exploits of this sometime civil engineer, mapmaker, surveyor and capable jack of many trades. Jane Eppinga, one of Flipper's biographers, succinctly described this intriguing individual "as an engineer, Spanish translator, Justice Department special agent, author, historian, and newspaper editor."

Besides many pursuits to earn a living, Flipper dabbled in real estate. Initially, he obtained a lot in Nogales, Arizona. Later, he bought another property on what became Nelson Street. He even served for a short time as a deputy post master, plus took part in local politics and temporarily stood in for a Nogales newspaper editor. What's more, he gathered and sometimes shared intelligence about the activities in Mexico during the turbulent revolutionary events south of the border. He even traveled to Washington, D.C., to share his findings.

The numerous references to Flipper typically lauded him, as well as in most instances referred to him by his rank, despite his dismissal from the U.S. Army. He bounced between Mexico, Arizona, California and the national capital, making him one of the best-traveled individuals in the territory. Not uncommon was Tucson's *Arizona Weekly Citizen*'s assessment on February 15, 1890: "He is a hard worker, and deserves his success."

As such, he was no stranger to this city. During one of several treks to there, he recounted that after entering the dining room of the Xavier Hotel, he spied West Point classmate Robert D. Read of the Tenth Cavalry. Soon after Flipper seated, the bigoted officer abruptly departed. Read walked out without waiting for his meal to be served.

INTERIM EVENTS

In fact, during 1898, another foe besides bigotry faced the Black troops. The explosion of USS *Maine* became a rallying cry and *casus belli* for the Spanish-American War and the subsequent utilization of Black regulars in the Philippines. Three years after returning from Cuba, the Tenth Cavalry and all the other U.S. Army mounted regiments underwent many changes. For instance, on February 2, 1901, Congress increased all cavalry and infantry units enlisted strength of a troop from 100 to 164 at the discretion of the president. Thereafter, for the next fifteen years, the size of the force varied annually from the ceiling of 100,000 because, until 1916, appropriations dictated the actual number of men. For instance, from 1902 to 1911, the total force averaged 65,616. The cavalry continued to form about one-fifth of the total. As of June 30, 1915, some 105,993 officers, NCOs and enlisted personnel served in the U.S. Army. Of these, 15,424 were assigned to the cavalry. More than seven full regiments, or about half of all the cavalry, served on the Mexican border, two regiments were deployed to the Philippines and one took station in Hawaii.

During these years, when there was greater interest in a more effective tactical organization of the army, cavalry received special consideration. In 1908, the army's chief of staff and various department commanders recommended an increase in the infantry and artillery and a reorganization of the cavalry along "more modern" lines.

This meant that during 1911 and 1912, the former twelve-troop regiment temporarily gave way to a half dozen troops by merging two troops into one. Additionally, experimental drill regulations followed European tactical models that called for double-rank formations focused on mounted action. As such, equestrian skills, better horses and heightened emphasis on the saber received increased attention. Nonetheless, proficiency with the rifle and ability to fight dismounted remained as requirements for well-trained troopers.

Following these new theories, in October 1914, all cavalry regiments received experimental service regulations for trial, which continued along the border during 1915 and 1916. After this period of experimentation, the vast majority of commanders supported a return to the old troop, squadron and regiment arranged in single rank. This meant that new drill and service regulations issued in 1916 retained the former organization and instruction for single-rank formations.

All these reform efforts took place during the upheaval in Mexico triggered in 1910–11 with the ousting of longtime dictatorial president Porfirio Díaz. The widespread unrest and violence in its southern neighbor caused concern in Washington, D.C., which eventually resulted in the concentration of most of the mounted and dismounted elements of the U.S. Army along the border. As part of this mobilization, the cavalry undertook patrol duties from the Rio Grande's mouth in Texas as far as to San Diego, California, covering a distance of approximately 1,700 miles. For maneuver purposes, units in the area formed into one division and two independent brigades.

One of the pair of latter organizations coupled with Ninth and Tenth Cavalry, plus a signal company, formed an independent brigade. This configuration proved short-lived, but the two regiments of Black horse soldiers continued on station in the Southwest. As counterrevolutionary activities continued in Mexico for several years from 1913, once more most U.S. cavalry regiments, consisting both of Black and white enlisted men, remained stretched out from the Gulf of Mexico almost to California.

BACK ON THE BORDER

As part of the concentration of U.S. military might, the Tenth Cavalry rejoined its comrades from the Ninth Cavalry, destined for monotonous missions in Arizona. As with the other four regiments in the post–Civil War Army composed entirely of Black enlisted men, discrimination persistently faced the Tenth Cavalry. Despite their laudable combat record in the Spanish-American War, men of the Tenth fell victim to increasing racism and hostility from many white Americans. Nevertheless, their performance won praise and the respect of the American public that gave rise to the regiment's early nickname, "the fighting Tenth Cavalry." Further, during this period, after sailing back from Cuba, the regiment did two tours in the Philippines; garrisoned Fort Robinson, Nebraska; and finally gained a posting in the East at Vermont. After spending the summer of 1913 at Winchester, Virginia, testing the proposed new cavalry drill regulations, the regiment returned briefly to its home for the previous several years, Fort Ethan Allen, Vermont. Soon, orders for the Tenth to transfer to the Southwest caused "a great scurrying around, especially among the junior officers," or so Captain George Brydges Rodney, a troop commander, recollected.

Although the Arizona press withheld making negative comments about the Black cavalrymen, as had been true shortly after the announcement that they would join in the mid-1880s Geronimo campaign, the relocation westward was not without its tribulations.

Leaving New England's frigid December weather, the regiment boarded a transport in New Jersey. Rodney recollected that they had a "pretty rough trip down to Galveston, Texas, and I felt very sorry for the horses because it was very cold, windy and rough."

After they arrived at Fort Huachuca, the men, mounts and families detrained followed by a march "over a rocky trail to the Post and the ladies and children drove that seven miles through a howling blizzard and a driving snowstorm." Once they reached their destination, Fort Huachuca, a troop from the Ninth Cavalry awaited them with the mounts that the Fourth, whom they were relieving, had left behind for their incoming replacements. The unexpected inclement weather necessitated fires to be "started in the empty houses but no other preparations for us had been made," Rodney revealed. This lack of arrangement for their arrival meant that Rodney and his family "slept on bedsprings laid flat on the floor and ate such food as an impromptu Chinese mess could provide. As a result one of my children got pneumonia and several grown people were laid up." The enlisted men fared no better.

One month later, on January 13, 1914, a second contingent of the Tenth departed the train at Huachuca siding. They made the seven-mile journey to the post, after which extracts from the regimental returns for 1914 offered a window into their duties. For instance, according to this source, during much of August, Headquarters Troop and Troops G, H, K and the Machine Gun Troop "engaged in target practice, drills and field training" and assorted garrison duties while stationed at Fort Huachuca. In like manner, Troop E headed to Nogales for border duty. In turn, Troops B and F were stationed at Camp Naco, Arizona, where they played similar roles to their counterparts detailed to Huachuca and Nogales, as was the case for Troop C, posted to Yuma. Only Troop L remained an "orphan" at Fort Apache. These troopers benefited from the peaceful, bucolic setting. As John Glass summarized in the Tenth's regimental history:

> The border stations were not at all attractive. The poor little shacks and 'dobes were eagerly sought for by officers and their wives. Naco was about as it is now, only more so. The usual border patrols were made along the line, enforcing neutrality, and keeping down gun-running. Every troop, during 1914, had a tour at Naco; Nogales was garrisoned by Troops A, E, G, H, M and the Machine Gun Platoon at different times during 1914. C troop was at Yuma April 23rd to September 6th; K and D took care of Forrest and Osborne.

From these bases of operation, elements of the regiment rotated on protective patrol duty; worked in tandem with civil law enforcement to interdict shipment of arms and ammunition into Mexico; occasionally offered medical assistance to casualties fleeing combat south of the border; and quelled violations of neutrality laws. Again, Tenth Cavalry captain Rodney rather wryly described the situation. Although he presented the story in a somewhat satiric manner, he clearly made his point:

> The Lieutenant takes his men to the hellhole where he's to stay and he calls his sergeant an' tells him: 'You take ten men today, Sergeant, and ride the border from Point o' Rocks to Saddlers' Wells. You'll take note of all the activities on the Mexican side of the line, especially any movement of troops and above all you'll see to it that the Neutrality Laws are strictly observed.

This tongue-in-cheek account portended more severe circumstances. In 1914, Villa's forces and Mexican government troops engaged in Naco, Sonora, sent both the Ninth and Tenth Cavalry to the unpredictable border. On October 7, the latter regiment's headquarters moved near the scene of combat. Soon, most the Tenth took up positions "in trenches and rifle pits all along the line, with machine guns all set for action," as recorded in John Glass's regimental history. In the process, stray fire from the warring Mexicans killed one trooper from the Ninth Cavalry and wounded another, both of whom served at Naco. The Tenth suffered casualties as well, but none died, while eight were wounded from the promiscuous shooting of the warring factions. As Glass indicated, "We had but eight men wounded." The Ninth also suffered some casualties. All recovered and returned to duty, except Private Leroy Bradford, Troop B. He would be discharged on surgeon's certificate of disability as result of his severe wound.

Fortunately, civilians in Naco, Arizona, were spared, although Mexican artillery struck many buildings in town that bore the marks for many years. Complicating matters, the cavalrymen experienced considerable difficulty "in holding back the crowds of visitors from Bisbee and Douglas who flocked to see the 'battles,' in automobiles, wagons and horseback," or so wrote Glass. After enduring dangerous duty, the conclusion allowed most of

During 1916, a squad of Tenth Cavalry troopers took up a position behind sandbags at Naco, Arizona. In the background stands one of the tents that served as temporary quarters before the military constructed more permanent facilities. *Courtesy the author.*

During 1920, Troop E, Tenth Cavalry, patrolled in the vicinity of Arivaca. This was one of many detachments dispatched to serve along the borderlands from Texas to California. *Courtesy the author.*

ap "E", 10th Cavalry
ficers seated in center,
t to right, Lt. Chace,
t. Ryder, Capt. Warren,
Heath. Arivaca, Ariz,
1918.

the troops to withdraw to their home base at Fort Huachuca. Some of them had spent ten months in the field.

During 1915, the troops from the Tenth, with the exception of Troop L, which remained a fixture at Fort Apache, rotated to various sites, including Arivaca, Harrison's Ranch, Fort Huachuca, La Osa, Lochiel, Osborn, Naco, Nogales, San Fernando, Sasabe and Yuma. In the process, as the regimental returns indicated, they performed "the usual garrison duties, engaged in target practice, drills, and field training." Units regularly rode out on patrols "in connection with the preservation of neutrality laws on the Mexican Border," as the regimental returns also reported. Late in the year, on November 21, two privates from Troop F of the Tenth Cavalry walked the border near Monument 117. They drew fire from the Mexican side of the border, which wounded Private Willie Norman. The following day, five armed Mexicans galloped into a Tenth Cavalry camp at the Santa Cruz River and shot at a detachment from Troop F. The Black cavalrymen responded with pistol fire. Possibly the troopers hit two Mexican raiders. On November 25, another bold incursion from Mexico struck an outpost of Troop F near Mascarena's Ranch. That same day, elements of Troop F occupied the western outskirts of the town of Nogales, Arizona.

Several troops of the Tenth also took up station in Nogales, having ridden from Naco on November 24. On November 25, one of the troops immediately reported to the border, with a second held close by in reserve. Then, the next day at 10:20 a.m., two troops occupied the boundary, while the other battalion served as possible reinforcements and remained in camp. Forty minutes later, Troop H withstood potshots from Sonora. The men returned fire until nearly 1:00 p.m. At that point, the exchange ceased. Two privates form Troop L sustained wounds but survived. A third soldier, white private Stephen D. Little from the Twelfth United States Infantry, succumbed to his wounds. On December 14, 1915, the U.S. Army ordered the camp at Nogales to be named in his honor. A few days earlier, with quiet returned to Nogales, Troops F and M withdrew for their return to Fort Huachuca.

PUNITIVE EXPEDITION OF 1916

Up to this point, Villa had enjoyed considerable popularity as a revolutionary fighting for his oppressed people. He even met with high-ranking U.S. civilian and military officials such as Brigadier John J.

As part of the 1916–17 Punitive Expedition into Mexico, Major Charles Young gained invaluable combat experience. It was during this pre–World War I period that he temporarily commanded Fort Huachuca, which at the time was an extremely rare assignment for an African American. *Courtesy National Archives and Records Administration.*

"Black Jack" Pershing, indicative of the stature he had gained during the Mexican Revolution. That esteem all but evaporated, however, after Villa's March 9, 1916 raid on the border town of Columbus, New Mexico. No longer a popular "Robin Hood" figure, Villa devolved into Public Enemy No. 1.

The United States mobilized with a vengeance. More than 100,000 regulars and national guardsmen flooded the border, including Black cavalrymen and infantrymen from Arizona who pushed south into Mexico as part of the spearhead of the Punitive Expedition under its field commander, none other than John Pershing. Among his subordinates was Charles Young, who would eventually take command of the Tenth U.S. Cavalry. Pershing inspected Young's troops at their camp in Dublan, Mexico. There, the ramrod straight Pershing could observe the Tenth's machine gunners going into action, given that this weapon would be employed for the first time in combat on the expedition, along with the inaugural combat use of mechanized vehicles (including armored cars), air power and modern communication systems.

Through backbreaking work of troops who dug dirt and formed adobe bricks so typical of construction in Mexico, they established a sprawling camp from which they could take to the field. In June 1916, one of the details consisting of Troops C and K of the Tenth Cavalry set out into the Mexican countryside. On June 23, they engaged in a desperate, devastating firefight with a well-positioned Mexican force who outnumbered them in Carrizal, Mexico. By the time the exchange ended, two officers and several enlisted men were dead, several wounded and most of the other survivors taken prisoner by the Mexican government garrison.

CHARLES YOUNG

In Mexico, Charles Young, the third and final Black U.S. Military Academy graduate of the nineteenth century, possessed a "good working knowledge of Latin, Greek, French, Spanish, and German," one of these languages proving useful on the border. By the time of the Mexican excursion, Young commanded a squadron of the Tenth. It was on this campaign that Young experienced his first and only incident of leading troops in combat. On April 1, 1916, the forward elements of the Tenth Cavalry under Colonel William C. Brown trotted south to Agua Caliente Ranch. Major Charles F. Young, in charge of Troops F and G, rode in the vanguard.

Around noon, Young's force located 150 *Villistas* near Agua Caliente. Once both of his troops arrived on the scene, the major maneuvered to flank the enemy on the left. Their charge routed the *Villistas*. Two Mexican dead remained on field, as did a machine gun and a pack saddle and other abandoned equipment. The squadron continued to pursue the scattered foe for a full two hours. Finally, the Mexicans found a strong position in a ravine, where they regrouped and fended off further attack until reinforcements arrived.

The next morning, the entire regiment once again took up the assault. In a maneuver similar to the one Young's command had executed the day before, he dispersed his troopers abreast. On Young's signal, the troopers blazed away with their Colt pistols, pouring fire on the *Villistas'* right flank, while other members of Tenth Cavalry supported the onslaught by firing machine guns over the heads of their comrades. The rapid-fire weapons and the determined charge on horseback scattered the defenders. The result was that Young's men never had to discharge their weapons. In the process, they had introduced a new technique: overhead machine gun fire.

IN ARIZONA AGAIN

Young's daring initiation and the release of the Tenth Cavalry POWs from the embarrassing debacle at Carrizal predated the early 1917 withdrawal of Pershing and the U.S. troops from Mexico, although they had not accomplished their mission to bring Villa to bay. Even during the Punitive Expedition, as Gerald Horne indicated in *Black and Brown: African Americans and the Mexican Revolution*, the mission of African American focused on

By 1918, elements of the Tenth Cavalry were clashing with a party of Yaqui raiders at Bear Valley. *Courtesy Arizona Historical Society.*

the policing of "a border repeatedly violated by revolutionaries and their allies," plus there were other duties, which even included interdicting drug trafficking and from time to time dealing with incursions by Yaquis who crossed illegally into *El Norte* often in quest of cattle and other supplies.

In the last-mentioned pursuit on January 9, 1918 approximately thirty members of this Indigenous group from Mexico opened fire on Troop E, Tenth Cavalry, in Tuscoso Canyon, which formed part of Bear Valley on the U.S. side of the border. Although outnumbered, the Yaquis proved adept guerrillas and "gave a good account of themselves." Eventually, they lost the skirmish. One of their band received a wound and subsequently died. The survivors were taken into custody, along with "a dozen or more rifles, some .30-30 Winchester carbines and German Mausers, lots of ammunition, powder and lead, and bullet molds." They were brought before the Federal District Court in Tucson, where a grand jury indicted nine of their number for "wrongfully, unlawfully and feloniously" exporting and taking arms from the United States. An understanding judge sentenced them to thirty days in the Pima County Jail, no doubt realizing that deportation would have resulted in their execution by the military governor of Sonora, which was bent on quelling the independent Yaquis—some in the government would have had no compunction in exterminating these proud people. As an aside, nearly a decade later, another group of Yaquis were apprehended but allowed to remain in the United States, eventually receiving recognition by the federal government leading to the establishment of their reservation in the environs of Tucson.

Responding to frequent raids from Mexico, another 1918 incident exploded. Civilians in the United States turned vigilante when they executed Mexicans thought to be marauders. During late August, in retaliation, the Battle of Ambos Nogales (the Battle of Both Nogales)—or, as it is known in Mexico, *La Batalla del 27 de Agosto* (the Battle of 27 August)—erupted between Mexican forces and elements of the U.S. Army. The latter force consisted of white soldiers from the Thirty-Fifth Infantry and Black troopers of the Tenth Cavalry under the overall command of Lieutenant Colonel Frederick J. Herman. The American soldiers and militia forces were stationed in Nogales, Arizona, and the Mexican regulars and armed Mexican militia garrisoned Nogales, Sonora. When the din of battle ceased, dead and wounded on both side of the "line" including twenty-nine Americans who sustained various stages of injury and seven dead U.S. soldiers. Among them was "Captain J.D. Hungerford at the head of a troop of the 10th Cavalry," who after he crossed the line east of town "was shot and instantly killed."

MEXICAN BORDER PROJECT

After the 1918 outbreak in Nogales, relative peace settled in the United States' neighboring republic. Continued concern for security along the international boundary, however, gave rise to an ambitious construction project. At first, the concept entailed the completion of a significant defensive line between Brownsville, Texas, at the Gulf of Mexico to Nogales, Arizona. Due to diverse environments, including several nearly impassable areas, practically all of which ran through arid areas and in some sections desert, subject to strong winds and sandstorms, the proposal presented many obstacles. Originally, the concept involved the building of a long road and parallel fence along the entire 1,200 miles. Prohibitive costs to build such an ambitious undertaking led to another approach designed by the U.S. Army and called the "Mexican Border Project."

As Bisbee's *Daily Review* divulged on June 7, 1919, the next iteration was a "huge barrier" but was not "a fence in the real sense of the word, though its purposes is the same." Instead, it was "a double row of cavalry patrol stations, barracks buildings and miscellaneous structures, stretching from Brownsville, Texas, on the Gulf of Mexico, to Arivaca, Ariz., on the edge of the great desert." At each station, typically one troop of cavalry, about one hundred men, would "be on guard all the time, patrolling the border between stations." As a "second line of defense," a projected dozen larger posts were "to serve as a base for four or five of the patrol stations on the boundary." These installations, said the reporter, "probably will be given the name 'forts,' but the war department emphasizes the fact that they will not be forts in reality, but merely army posts, such as Ft. Bliss, Ft. Ringgold and the other 'forts' already on the border."

The completed system had the capacity of housing ten thousand soldiers. Their primary purpose, continued the news article, entailed "defense against the elements, and not against the Mexicans. It is admitted, however that the patrol stations are for the purpose of guarding the border against invasions by bandits, and cattle thieves." The only opening in the seamless corridor stood at the "desert wastes between Nogales and Yuma."

As noted in the after-action report for the project written by Lieutenant Colonel F.G. Chamberlain, who headed up the endeavor as the constructing quartermaster:

> *As these troops could not efficiently patrol districts far removed from their stations, or remain sheltered in tents for any great period of time without a decided decrease in morale, the Assistant Secretary of War on Feb. 28, 1919, approved the necessary construction to adequately house and otherwise provide for them.*
>
> *These posts and camps were, in some cases, developments of existing posts, of former frontier posts long since abandoned and turned over to the Department of the Interior; others were entirely new layouts on leased land, adaptable to the purpose on account of good sanitary possibilities and strategic position.*

The U.S. Army allocated more than $8,700,000 in funds and material for this ambitious enterprise. Work commenced on nearly four dozen posts and sub-posts and met with various degrees of success. Some projects reached fruition, as predicted by Bisbee's *Daily Review* May 14, 1919 issue. The paper pointed out the benefit to the local economy. Increased troop strengths meant more local military expenditures. Moreover, the military proposed "plans and specifications…for one infirmary, one recreation hall, four barracks, two mess halls, lavatories, one bakery, four officers' quarters, six non-commissioned officers' quarters, stables for 60 animals, two blacksmith shops, one hay shed, one grain shed, a corral with fencing and a warehouse with railroad tracks leading to it."

Similarly, military authorities envisioned several improvements at Douglas such as "two large warehouses and 36 officers' quarters and a field laundry. Bids will be opened at 10 a. m. on June 2, 1919, and must arrive at the office of the constructing quartermasters, Mexican border projects, Camp Travis, Texas, previous to that date. Blank forms for the proposals can be obtained by writing to the constructing quartermaster." The reporter ended with another fiscal note, writing, "The amount of money involved in the project amounts to millions and the increase of the military forces will embrace practically one-third of the contemplated revision of America's peace strength army to 500,000 men."

As the August 9, 1919 issue of Bisbee's *Daily Review* testified, the construction quartermaster at that camp said that the "work on the new barracks there has been delayed on account of curtailment of all construction work along the Mexican border. He expects, however, that the tieup from 'higher up' will soon straighten out sufficiently to enable him to push along the extensive work planned." Continuing, the writer underscored that "water systems go with all these camps and sewer and lighting systems in most of them." This included the Naco post, where work had not commenced as yet for the "35 adobe buildings and water and sewer systems."

Conversely, the other facility built of adobe, the Castolon army compound in the Big Bend country of Texas, never reached completion, nor would the post be occupied by troops. Regardless of individual status, after Herbert Hoover replaced Calvin Coolidge as president, progress halted. Some sites remained, while others such as at Douglas, Naco and Lochiel closed. One officer from the Tenth, Captain Clarence Richmond, recalled orders to proceed to the last-mentioned site "and wash it off the face of the earth; add concrete footings to the temporary target range [at the fort]; take the pumping plant and the light plant and bring them on up here and relocate them on the target range."

The relatively peaceful situation not only meant the closure of some installations, but rumors also circulated that the Tenth Cavalry would be transferred from Fort Huachuca to Nogales, while the Twenty-Fifth Infantry would move to the Philippine Islands. In 1921, the Bisbee Chamber of Commerce went on record to oppose the proposal.

Troop movements were preempted. In fact, elements of the regiment continued their patrols. Because of its familiarity with the region, a detachment from the Tenth Cavalry seemed a likely choice as part of a military mapping expedition of segments of southeastern Arizona. This endeavor started in 1922. Three years later, some enlisted men still had spare time at Fort Huachuca to star as cavalrymen extras in a 1925 western film about the Indian Wars. They played troopers of the 1880s, while the post's Indian scouts and their relatives assumed the parts of Apache warriors.

REVOLUTION RETURNS

All seemed well until a new source of tensions arose. Between 1923 and 1929, unrest once more rocked the country. Over a half dozen years, various opposing forces periodically challenged the national government in Mexico City. To begin with, President Alvaro Obregón faced opposition from fellow Sonoran and former ally Felipe Adolfo de la Huerta Marcor. For three months, De La Huerta led what ended as a failed revolt. He claimed that he acted in resistance to the president's corruption. Obregón weathered the assault and temporarily left office.

Obregón eventually returned to the Presidential Palace. Before he did so, a powerful movement erupted in the wake of actions by the interim chief executive, Plutarco Elías Calles. As one of Calles's early activities, he issued an executive decree to enforce Article 130 of the Mexican constitution. He intended to curb the long-standing power of the Catholic Church. In reaction, armed resistance erupted against Calles and gave rise to the so-called Cristero War (*La Guerra Cristera*), also known as the Cristero Rebellion (*La Cristiada*). Three years of brutal battles ensued.

Nearly simultaneously, the often-oppressed Yaqui people in Sonora initiated a guerrilla war that required Calles to dispatch more than half of the federal army to put down the insurgents. Among the Yaquis, Ramon Yucupicio gained prominence. His accomplishments included assuming command of the rebel forces fighting federal troops at Naco, Sonora.

When sparring began at Naco, to protect the Naco-Bisbee water supply and in response to a request made by local citizens of Naco and Bisbee, the U.S. military dispatched five hundred troops. Contingents from the Tenth Cavalry at Fort Huachuca and elements from the Twenty-Fifth Infantry sent from Douglas arrived. They mounted machine guns and were prepared to protect lives and property of Americans. Meanwhile, officers and enlisted men observed the contest along with townsmen. Fortunately, at the outset, the violence did not spread northward. By 1929, that good fortune had ended.

In early April, the situation changed. First of all, Patrick Murphy, an Irish American barnstorming and crop duster pilot, offered his service to the

Cristero rebels. Arming his biplane with bombs, he took to the air determined to dislodge the defending federals from their trenches. His inaccurate effort resulted in the first bomb landing in Arizona. At 7:45 a.m. on April 2, 1929, he had the dubious distinction of launching the first aerial attack on American soil. During the next several days, he failed to improve his aim. Time after time, his bombing raid hit unintended targets in Naco, Arizona. In the process, he shattered windows as well as damaged other buildings on the American side of the border. He damaged a garage, the Phelps-Dodge Mercantile and the Haas Pharmacy. One of his misguided missiles even smashed into the post office. This made Murphy's rash acts a federal offense. The worst damage was the total destruction of a Dodge touring car.

Two days later, Tenth Cavalry private John Finezee, a member of Troop K, took a round in the chest. A skirmish followed after some of his fellow troopers discovered a number of grenades or dynamite on the American side of the border near a tunnel of the Northern Pacific Railway line. An American cavalry patrol challenged a group of nearby rebels, who, in turn, responded with a volley. Finezee fell in the melee, although he recovered. His comrades' return fire drove the Mexicans back into Sonora.

Bullets also crossed the line during this attack, striking a Mexican woman and her small daughter in Naco, Arizona. Scarcely a building on the American side escaped being struck by stray shots, which along with Murphy's bombs left visible scars for many years.

As part of the clash, Yucupicio's Yaqui cavalry poured across the border into the United States. They only encroached for a few yards before a reinforced Tenth Cavalry patrol under Lieutenant R.W. Curtis drove the invaders back across the border into Mexico.

Likewise, violence existed in Nogales's neighborhood. According to Nogales's *International* for March 15, 1929, the commanding officer of the Twenty-Fifth Infantry at Camp Little dispatched a patrol to interdict a supposed Mexican raid on an American ranch. The paper stated: "In case of a battle across the line the United States troops will move to the border and take positions in Nogales, Arizona, overlooking Nogales, Sonora, it is reported. There they will be prepared to protect American lives and property in case any bullets from the hostile forces fly into this city."

Colonel A.M. Shipp, who commanded Camp Little, sought reinforcements from the Tenth. Their presence proved unnecessary. They arrived in Nogales around the time of a cessation of hostilities as the result of a truce between the warring Mexicans.

SPORTS, BASEBALL AND BANDS

While the Tenth Cavalry only occasionally faced Mexican revolutionaries and bandits, as proved true for all four Buffalo Soldier regiments posted to Arizona, more frequently they encountered civilians in the region through music and sports, such as track meets and field as well as baseball games. Often, Tenth Cavalry teams challenged local rivals in Bisbee, Douglas, Nogales and elsewhere. Likewise, they took on military teams, mostly Black foot soldiers from the Twenty-Fifth Infantry, as well as white doughboys from the Thirty-Fifth Infantry.

In fact, many men from the Tenth, including the regimental band, periodically frequented Bisbee's venerable Warren Park. The town's *Tribune* for August 3, 1918, offered a telling recap of one of these encounters that featured "the boys of Machine Gun Troop" who despite the loss of the game drew praise from the reporter. His coverage revealed:

> *The band came with them and gave to the people, of Bisbee the best music of the season. Hundreds of people came from the surrounding cities. Warren Park had one of the largest crowds it has had this season, due to the record of the boys in khaki.*

As a means of maintaining physical fitness as well as contributing to elan, sporting events included track meets, such as this one held in 1925 by the Tenth Cavalry. *Courtesy the author.*

Around 1915, these combined Fifth and Tenth Cavalry troopers played as "herald" trumpeters. They not only demonstrated their musical abilities, even on horseback, but they also constituted a rare occasion of Black and white soldiers serving together as integrated. *Courtesy Fort Huachuca Museum.*

All four Buffalo Soldier regiments would gain enviable stature for their athletics, such as these proud members of Troop I, Tenth Cavalry's baseball team, who boasted an impressive win record in the early 1920. *Courtesy Fort Huachuca Museum.*

Quite a number of the soldiers of the Tenth Cavalry remained in Bisbee a day or so after the ball game Sunday. Mr. Walter J. Stewart of the U.S. Tenth Cavalry spent a few days in Bisbee after playing in the band Sunday. He walked into a confectionery store on Brewery Gulch and asked to be served. The proprietor became very much distressed and finally said:

"I am sorry, but we can't serve colored people." Mr. Stewart asked him several questions; what his name was, etc., and before Mr. Stewart and his young lady companion left, they had been served free of charge. We do not know whether the proprietor was frightened or whether he just changed his mind. The last thing Mr. Stewart was heard to say as be came out of the door was: "No colored man ever shot a president. This uniform means the same thing a white man's does."

Once again, on June 29, 1919, throughout nine innings, the Tenth's sluggers kept their comrades in the band and other fans on the edges of their seats. This time, they faced skillful opponents from Lowell, Arizona, who bested them. The exchange was not without issues, or so stated the *Bisbee Daily Review*. A recap of the match lamented that "an otherwise fine exhibition was marred, unfortunately, by constant 'beefing' by the players on both sides. That such tactics are not popular with the fans was evidenced by the demonstration of disapproval from the stands which greeted the protests made on the field." Adding to the ill will, "the umpiring, on both sides, was of a variety to call forth the ire" of both teams and many in the bleachers. Some sources, then and now, maintained that this contested competition contributed to a rare confrontation between law enforcement and troopers from the Tenth.

"RACE RIOT"

Before that game, however, a previous incident set the tone for a future confrontation. Four members of the Tenth Cavalry, stationed at Naco, ended up in the camp's guardhouse. They supposedly dared Bisbee police officers Wednesday to arrest them. Local law enforcement accommodated them after the quartet brandished automatics and pointed them at Officers Sherrill and Gannon.

Several months later, during the evening of July 3, a tussle once more marred the usually quiet presence of Black soldiers in Bisbee. In town to lead the next day's Fourth of July celebrations, about three hundred off-duty Buffalo Soldiers enjoyed a respite from their military assignments. Some of them passed the time in a segregated "club in upper Brewery Gulch, known as the Silver Leaf club," or so said the *Arizona Republican* for July 4, 1919. The headline blared, "TENTH TROOPS ENGAGE BISBEE POLICE. Four Wounded Including Deputy Sherriff, in Race Riot—One Negro Soldier Reported Seriously Injured." In addition, the report continued:

> *The riot was precipitated at 10 o'clock in the evening when George Sullivan, white, military policeman of the Nineteenth United States infantry stationed at Douglas, was passing by a negro club in upper Brewery Gulch, known as the Silver Leaf club, while on duty. Five negro cavalrymen, according to Sullivan and other witnesses, made a taunting remark as he passed. Seeing they were intoxicated, Sullivan says, he told them they had best go home.*
>
> *The negroes, Sullivan says, drew revolvers, knocked him down, and took his own weapon from him. Several civilians started to his aid and the negroes fled.*
>
> *The negroes refused to disarm at the request of the officers and left. The officers then started out for a general disarming of all negroes, in the course of which exchanges of shots were frequent.*
>
> *A Mexican woman, Mrs. Teresa Leyvas of Bisbee, 19 years of age, was shot in the right side and head from one of the fusillades in the Depot. Doctors who removed the bullet have pronounced the wound not serious.*

After the 1906 outbreak in Brownsville that resulted in the dismissal of nearly an entire battalion of soldiers from the Twenty-Fifth Infantry and, eleven years later, a "mutiny" of men from the Twenty-Fourth Infantry, then stationed at Camp Logan in Houston, Texas, this incident received considerable attention. Adding to the mix, in 1919, nearly two dozen racial flare-ups known as the "Red Summer" witnessed widespread national discord between whites and Blacks. Typically, the former group started the upheavals. In turn, the latter victims fought back. Sadly, deaths, injuries and property destruction ensued as a result.

In the midst of this chaos, the majority of the white officers were present at a nearby dance. After news reached them, the regimental commander sent a lieutenant and half a dozen enlisted men to quell the outbreak. The number of peacekeepers proved highly inadequate. Later military investigations faulted the regiment's commanding colonel for not reacting sooner and likewise failing to order out a larger response force. Also, U.S. Army investigators subsequently concluded from eyewitness citizen statements that the civilian police were responsible for the majority of shootings. According to one military intelligence officer's review of the matter, in particular, Deputy Sheriff Joseph Hardwick was "probably the man who shot every man who was injured in the firing."

On July 27, 1919, the *Tombstone Epitaph* further indicated, "A fair example of the treatment Tenth cavalry soldiers received in Bisbee was the wounding of one soldier three times as he ran around the railroad station; a man shot in the back as he ran after a detachment of Tenth cavalry being marched down the street under an officer, and men clubbed and beaten after they had surrendered their pistols."

Even so, fourteen Tenth cavalrymen were jailed. They briefly remained in custody. At last, the regimental commander appeared on the scene. The local authorities released them without further repercussions. Remarkably, the next morning, the Tenth took its place at the head of the Independence Day parade.

LAWLESS ELEMENTS

This atypical outbreak ran contrary to the norm whereby the cavalrymen would "conduct themselves in a splendid manner when in town," as the *Bisbee Daily Review* revealed on October 21, 1914. Nonetheless, the Tenth, as with any group, had its share of lawless members. Murders, violent assault including rape, theft, illegal liquor procurement during Prohibition, drunken and disorderly conduct, extortion and the gamut of infractions great and small existed. As in other regiments, these outbursts occurred at such places as White City adjacent to Fort Huachuca.

An example from late 1915 involved a trooper named Jesse Loveless, who was convicted of rape committed on the Fort Huachuca reservation. His crime led to a sentence of life imprisonment at Fort Leavenworth. Another Tenth Cavalry soldier sent to Leavenworth, a native of Washington, Georgia, David Wingfield, joined the regiment in December 1913. The athletic private stood at five-foot-ten and weighed 168 pounds. He claimed to be an expert cavalryman who was a proficient equestrian, rifleman and expert pistol shot. Wingfield somewhat proved his proficiency with a pistol nearly two years after joining the Tenth. During December 1915, evidently he formed part of a trio, all of whom frequented a prostitute working out of the infamous

Troops stopped for refreshments at Carmichael's general store, which provided a more wholesome respite than some of the other unsavory civilian establishments that existed near Fort Huachuca. *Courtesy Fort Huachuca Museum.*

White City. One payday, he and another of the other members of this *ménage à quatre*, a Corporal Duncan, had been drinking. For an unknown reason, the two men leveled their pistols at each other. Duncan's .32-caliber struck Wingfield in the right wrist, upper back and left hip. Wingfield's aim proved more lethal. He struck Duncan in the chest, killing him.

Early the next year, the January 7, 1916 edition of Bisbee's *Daily Review* recounted that the officers at the fort "wanted him dealt with by the civil authorities." Their request went unheeded. They could not secure support from the civilian court. This meant a general court-martial followed, which resulted in a sentence of ten years' imprisonment. Sent to Leavenworth in May 1916, the twenty-two-year-old had not yet fully recovered. Even so, he joined the prison's baseball team, the Booker T's. Eight games later, his performance as a right-handed second baseman and pitcher brought about an unusual turn of events. He secured a release from Leavenworth to become one of four inmates paroled to play with the Negro League! During his first season, Wingfield appeared on the roster of the Dayton Marcos. The next year, he rotated to the Detroit Stars, where he remained until joining his final club, the Toledo Tigers, where he made his last appearance in 1923.

While Wingfield was spending his last full year free, another victim of White City, Private Edward L. Sappington, Troop B, Tenth Cavalry, "was shot through the head and the heart, while several bullets struck him in various other parts of the body," as the *Bisbee Daily Review* indicated on November 4, 1919. A board of Tenth Cavalry officers convened, but they and civilian authorities never ascertained who killed Sappington.

Following up on the story, the *Tombstone Epitaph* of November 9, 1919, added that Sappington's remains went by train to his hometown in Kansas City. The *Epitaph* concluded, "This adds another death to the toll of White City, the resort which opens its doors as fast as it can be put out of business by the county and military authorities. Many times have the conductors of this resort been arrested and to leave the county, but soon afterward it is again running full blast under a new head. It is a menace to the Fort."

While Sappington's remains traveled eastward, one of his comrades confessed that he killed his fellow cavalrymen. It was an old story. Private Hook, as a reporter from Flagstaff's *Coconino Sun* wrote on November 14, 1919, "had trouble over affections of a Mexican girl, one of the inmates of the Pugh place." Because his crime took place off the military reservation, he was to be tried in the Superior Court at Tombstone.

Not surprisingly, this was not the last White City homicide. On July 6, 1920, the *Arizona Republican* illustrated another example of fatal aggression.

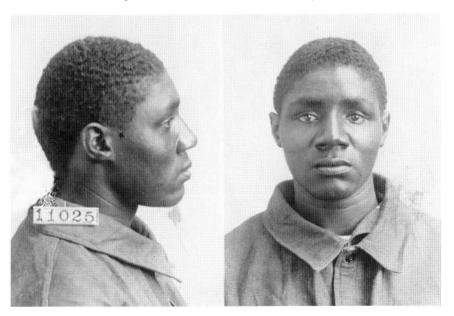

Tried and convicted of murder, former Tenth Cavalry private Paul Wingfield headed to Leavenworth Penitentiary as a prisoner. Soon thereafter, he received a parole in order to become a baseball player in the Negro Leagues! *Courtesy National Archives and Records Administration.*

Aerial view of Fry/White City in 1939, two years before the further growth of the dens of vice during World War II. *Courtesy Fort Huachuca Museum.*

Five enlisted men from the Tenth Cavalry "were bound over to await the action of the superior court on the charge of murder." They killed a Black civilian during a "gambling game at White City." The men claimed that they gunned down "the civilian in a spirit of revenge, although investigation by officers proved the motive was robbery."

Fortunately, most men of the Tenth faithfully discharged their duties without straying. More typical were steadfast men such as H. Sessions, who soon after the conclusion of the Spanish-American War enlisted in the Tenth U.S. Volunteer Infantry. After his days with the "immunes" (because of a stereotype that Black soldiers were immune to tropical diseases and climate), Sessions reenlisted. This time he joined Troop G, Tenth Cavalry, where he remained for seventeen years, including service at Naco, where he earned a service ribbon awarded for his participation in the defense of that community prior to participation in the Punitive Expedition into Mexico. After twenty-five years of faithful performance, First Sergeant Sessions received his much-deserved honorable discharge along with a regimental review by the Twenty-Fourth Infantry, with which he served during his last years in uniform.

THE SABER RETIRES

Over his quarter of a century of service, Sessions, like the majority of his comrades, spent much of the time occupied in an array of martial tasks. Among their routines, the Tenth Cavalry and its brother regiments engaged in regular maneuvers. By the early 1930s, airplanes and armored vehicles had emerged in ever-increasing numbers as part of these exercises. Indeed, airpower and mechanization increasingly eroded the need for horse cavalry. Beginning in 1921, a significant army-wide reorganization that evolved through 1940 witnessed the incremental decline of the Ninth and Tenth Cavalry regiments troop strengths, along with major reductions of the Twenty-Fourth and Twenty-Fifth Infantry regiments. Ultimately, Black soldiers constituted less than 2 percent of both the U.S. Army and National Guard's total force, which represented a significant decline from the past.

On August 29, 1931, the *Nogales International* captured the drawdown on the border, the decline of horse cavalry as a combat arm and the reduction of African Americans personnel in the U.S. Army. The headline read, "10TH CAVALRY WILL LEAVE FT. HAUCHUCA. Historic Regiment to Be Scattered to Three Places." As a result of decades of duty periodically from the mid-1880s through the early 1930s, the regiment had become a mainstay in Arizona. Now the unit splintered, with elements heading to the U.S. Military

On February 11, 1911, the Tenth Cavalry adopted a regimental emblem that displayed a bison. More than a decade later, the U.S. Army approved a distinctive unit insignia consisting of a bison racing right or left (the badge is worn in pairs). The leftward-facing buffalo represents the westward movement. A scroll below bears the Tenth's motto, "Ready and Forward."

Academy in New York; Fort Riley, Kansas; and to Fort Myer, Virginia. In turn, their support elements remained behind, as did the Twenty-Fifth Infantry. This move all but ended the unit's combat effectiveness. A furor emerged among the troops, the NAACP and others, who opposed "[t]he possible dissolution of this famous army unit, which is the pride of the Negro race. has forcibly stirred colored leaders and organizations everywhere and they are protesting the order. President Hoover is urged to countermand the order. Several colored leaders stated this week 'Hoover is sure to lose the Negro vote should the Tenth Cavalry he disbanded,'" according to Seattle, Washington's *Northwest Enterprise* on September 3, 1931.

By October 14, 1931, Nogales's *International* had confirmed that the final element of Tenth Cavalry left Fort Huachuca. Rumors also ran that the post itself would be closed, a possibility that drew negative responses from citizens in Douglas, Nogales and elsewhere, who sought protection along the border. The plan envisioned deploying the cavalry's second squadron to West Point, transferring the headquarters troop and first squadron to Fort Riley and posting the machine gun troop to Fort Myer, Virginia. In turn, much to the chagrin of numerous residents of Douglas and Nogales, Twenty-Fifth Infantry battalions assigned to Camps Jones and Little were rotated to join the remaining battalion at Fort Huachuca.

With that, the Tenth Cavalry, whose regimental motto was "Ready and Forward," saw its last sunset in Arizona.

CHAPTER 3

TWENTY-FOURTH INFANTRY

"SEMPER PARATUS"

ORIGINS

In 1869, yet another army-wide reorganization significantly reduced the number of infantry regiments that had been established three years earlier. This included the consolidation of the former Thirty-Eighth and Forty-First Infantry regiments under the redesignation of the Twenty-Fourth U.S. Infantry. A pair of well-known officers, both veterans of the Civil War, obtained colonelcy and lieutenant colonelcy positions. They were Ranald S. Mackenzie and William R. Shafter, respectively. From 1869 through 1880, they served in Texas. By autumn of 1880, orders had transferred them to Indian Territory (Oklahoma), where they served variously at Forts Supply, Reno, Sill and Cantonment on the north fork of the Canadian River, while some elements remained in Texas at Fort Elliott. Through June 1888, the Twenty-Fourth led a quiet, stable existence. In fact, throughout its nearly first two decades of existence, it saw no campaigning.

ARIZONA AND NEW MEXICO

During the summer of 1888, after it reported to the Department of Arizona, this undisturbed status quo continued. At that juncture, regimental headquarters, the band and three companies settled at Fort Bayard, New

Mexico. Early on, the remaining companies rotated between Forts Grant and Thomas, as well as the Apache reservation at San Carlos, this site being the least desirable from the standpoint of climate and amenities, such as they were, at a frontier garrison. While lacking niceties, the duty was not especially taxing or dangerous. To ensure that the soldiers were not lulled into complacency, in August 1889, the departmental commander ordered the establishment of camps of instruction. In the cases of maneuvers at Forts Apache, Stanton, Thomas, Wingate and San Carlos, because of "the proximity of Indians" to these garrisons, he instructed commanders of these posts always to maintain "a sufficiently strong force" behind when leaving for field maneuvers.

WHAM PAYROLL ROBBERY

Although these precautions were unnecessary, a few men from the Twenty-Fourth faced other adversaries. During spring of 1889, U.S. Army paymaster Major Joseph Washington Wham set out with $48,345.10 in heavy $5, $10 and $20 gold and silver pieces. That amount dwindled after the garrisons at Bowie and Grant received their due, but the remaining $29,000 tipped the scales at upward of 450 pounds! The remaining weighty treasure was pay for the troops at Fort Thomas, along with the soldiers at San Carlos and Fort Apache.

Completing his first disbursement at Fort Grant without incident, the major and his civilian clerk, W.T. Gibson, boarded a jostling army conveyance referred to as an "ambulance." In addition, a specially fitted out "Dougherty Wagon" allowed five of the Twenty-Fourth infantrymen assigned to the patrol to view in opposite directions and additionally to watch over the safe, carried in the center of the wagon bed. A mounted detachment from the Tenth Cavalry completed the escort. This detail consisted of two noncommissioned officers from the Twenty-Fourth. Sergeant Benjamin Brown and Corporal Isaiah Mays had immediate command of this mixed contingent of ten enlisted men from both the infantry and cavalry, bound for Fort Thomas.

All went well until the driver suddenly halted when he came upon a large boulder obstructing the roadway. The escort alighted to remove the barrier. As they did so, the well-positioned robbers fired a volley of about twenty rounds. The fusillade forced the soldiers to retreat. During the ensuing

The U.S. Army acknowledged Corporal Isaiah Mays with the Medal of Honor for his bravery during the Wham payroll fight. Despite his exemplary service, he was buried without recognition of his deed. Decades later, he received a well-deserved reburial at Arlington National Cemetery. *Courtesy Library of Congress.*

exchange, eight of the men, including Sergeant Brown, sustained wounds. For his heroism under fire, Brown, along with Corporal Mays, received Medals of Honor. The U.S. Army recognized the valor of eight other defenders with Certificates of Merit (which were replaced by the Distinguished Service Medal in 1918 and by the Distinguished Service Cross in 1934).

Upon initial investigation, the holdup positions revealed two or more spent cartridges. Soon afterward, civilian law enforcement and military patrols, such as one from Troop K, Tenth Cavalry, went in pursuit. They took eleven men, who mostly resided near or in the Mormon community of Pima, into custody. Eight of those apprehended by law enforcement stood trial. At the hearing, the major's testimony appeared in the November 15, 1889 issue of Tucson's *Arizona Daily Citizen*. He stated that the assailants fired from "natural forts" that covered both sides of the road. Wham then recounted:

> *When the flank-firing began the escort ran down the hill; I remained with only Private [Julius] Harrison; thought Harrison killed a man; he was shot and then started to run; I was then to the left along alone; called to*

the Corporal to return, but he did not do so, when I followed them; I saw a robber raise from behind a rock showing himself to his waist; who spoke and told me to go off to the left, which I did; I left the rock to rally the escort; had I remained—I would have been killed.

Despite eyewitness accounts and other evidence, the court released all the accused after a verdict of not guilty exonerated them. Evidently, they were free to spend the spoils because none of the haul was recovered. The exploits of Brown, Mays and their comrades who made the stand at "Bloody Run" would be forgotten until decades later.

FINAL "CAMPAIGNS"

The Twenty-Fourth remained in Arizona for several more years. This included periodic rotations to San Carlos Reservation. Some transfers also occurred, including one in 1892. Companies A, B, C and H took station at Fort Huachuca through 1896. The remaining companies and regimental headquarters continued at Fort Bayard, New Mexico. These final years proved tranquil. In fact, the regimental history compiled by William G. Muller recorded, "There was, however, no fighting to speak of. The redoubtable 'Apache Kid' was out terrorizing the miners and settlers, who were about as bad as the Indians."

Nevertheless, on occasion, elements of the regiment left the quiet of Fort Huachuca for field service. For example, in 1894, when union strikers took control of the property of the Atchison, Topeka and Santa Fe and the Denver Gulf Railroads, marshals sent against the laborers also fell into the hands of the strikers, who disarmed the several dozen lawmen. In response, Sergeant Benjamin Brown and Company C, as well as Company H, mobilized to protect railroad assets in such places such as Trinidad, Colorado. After two months on this special duty, these contingents returned to Fort Huachuca.

During November 1895, Companies A and B left Fort Huachuca on a practice march. They camped on the flat north of town, east of the railway. Curious local residents came to the temporary camp as an audience. Many of these onlookers saw the Krag rifle, adopted in the early 1890s for infantrymen, that replaced black powder .40-70-caliber cartridges with smokeless powder .30-40 ammunition.

Company I, 24th Infantry at volley-firing. Fort Thomas, Ariz.

A company of the Twenty-Fourth Infantry qualified at Fort Thomas's firing range in the late 1880s. *Courtesy the author.*

Less than a year later, in 1896, Company C once more left the fort for deployment to the border. In August, the infantrymen responded to the seizure of the Mexican Custom House by filibusters, who supposedly staged in Arizona. The foot soldiers again took up station in the vicinity of Nogales, Sonora. As a result of this escapade, a trio of Mexican civilians, along with seven filibusters, died. In the wake of this violence, reports that the marauders had headed north into Arizona and were making their way toward Tubac meant that again two companies of the Twenty-Fourth Infantry, one of which included the ever-ready Sergeant Brown, set out to capture the fleeing force. Rumors that fifty Native Americans likewise threatened Nogales, Arizona, resulted in entraining the infantrymen for rapid arrival at that border town. Additional reinforcements from the white Seventh Cavalry took to the saddle toward Harshaw, Arizona, where they sought to bring the surviving filibusters into custody.

While the horse soldiers rode on their mission, around midnight of August 12, the train bearing the infantrymen pulled into Nogales. By August 13, they along with more troopers from the Seventh Cavalry had been sent from Forts Huachuca and Grant continued to Tubac as a reassuring martial presence.

In contrast, at Nogales, pandemonium reigned. Armed ad hoc vigilante groups took up positions to protect residences and businesses. During the

Apache prisoners, overseen by both white and Black soldiers at the San Carlos guardhouse, illustrated the complex, diverse population of Arizona Territory. *Courtesy the author.*

Interior of Guardhouse at San Carlos, Ariz. 1885.

Right: A private from Company B, Twenty-Fourth Infantry, spent some of his thirteen-dollars-per-month pay at Tucson photographer Henry Buehman's business for a full-length portrait. *Courtesy Arizona Historical Society, azB11258.*

Below: During the 1890s, Fort Huachuca's commissary stored foodstuffs for the Twenty-Fourth. *Courtesy National Archives and Records Administration.*

Many regiments housed their horses and mules at Fort Huachuca's stables, including the Tenth Cavalry. *Courtesy National Archives and Records Administration.*

chaos, the commanding colonel of the expedition discovered that Yaqui Indians, long at odds with the Mexican government, had staged the attack to obtain weapons and supplies. Townsmen in both Nogales, Sonora, and Arizona rallied to their own defense until the companies of the Twenty-Fourth fanned out to restore order and ready themselves for a feared possible attack by the Yaquis.

Intent on quelling violations of neutrality laws or apprehending individuals who lent aid to those who did so, a patrol from the Tenth arrested three Yaqui Indians and one Mexican national in Tubac. Shortly thereafter, a larger force gathered for a march to the village of Greaterville, believed to be the hideout of the filibusters. That intelligence proved false. With that, the department commander received a telegram from the field recommending the withdrawal of the units and a recall to their respective duty stations. By early September, all but one company left behind as a precautionary measure at Nogales, Arizona, had complied.

In response to the performance of the Twenty-Fourth Infantry and their comrades from brother units, the department commander's annual report for 1896 noted that "every rumor and clew [*sic*] calculated to throw light upon the movements of the raiders were thoroughly investigated and the entire country in a radius of nearly 70 miles east, north, and west of Nogales was completely covered." In the process, details from the Twenty-Fourth and other regiments serving in Arizona and New Mexico covered 42,457 miles, although in the main most of the marches relied on horse soldiers.

During the majority of the 1890s, however, the battalion of the Twenty-Fourth concentrated on performing morning ablutions (including bathing twice a week), donning uniforms and then setting down to a communal breakfast by 7:30 a.m. Most of the enlisted men were engaged in fatigue duties through 12:15 p.m., when they returned to the mess halls for a second meal. About forty-five minutes later, they resumed fatigue details or attended various types of training through 4:30 p.m. Some fifteen minutes later, they drilled and stood from guard mount followed by a brief return for barracks and a final meal at 5:30 p.m. Tattoo sounded at 9:00 p.m., followed by the haunting bugle notes of taps. Given the garrison's relatively large number of troops, enlisted men drew guard duty on average about every ten days, as part of some of the details assigned to them in addition to the usual schedule.

Other deviations from the norm often included target practice and marksmanship competitions. Many men of the regiment excelled in this key area of weapon proficiency. In another case, one noncommissioned officer and seventeen privates left post for La Noria, Arizona, as a temporary escort to the International Boundary Commission to relieve a detachment from Company C, Twenty-Fourth Infantry, previously detached from Fort Huachuca for the same purpose. Likewise, on occasion, practice marches broke the daily regimen. One such outing, also in 1892, entailed a respectable twenty-five-mile hike in a single day, which was no mean accomplishment given that the men carried their rifles, ammunition and weighty field kit. That same year, Company C compiled the most impressive record in the battalion, accumulating 310 miles in eighteen days.

Four years later, a sergeant and private from Company B and four men of Company H, Twenty-Fourth Infantry, departed Fort Huachuca for the Chiricahua Mountains, where they spent thirty days on a recreational hunting excursion that also offered a change of diet from the military ration. During the respite, they killed eighteen white-tailed deer and a silver-tip bear.

Such forays partially helped alleviate "[t]hree related problems of garrison life…boredom, drunkenness, and desertion," as Bruno Rolak underscored in his *History of Fort Huachuca*. A billiard room; a game room for checkers, chess and cards (no betting allowed); and a reading room fitted out with various periodicals and books further helped alleviate the doldrums.

Barracks afforded little solitude and minimal living space, as these men from the Twenty-Fourth Infantry well knew in the 1890s. *Courtesy National Archives and Records Administration.*

A two-story barracks at Fort Huachuca housed Twenty-Fourth infantry soldiers. Later, the Tenth Cavalry and other units called these humble quarters home. *Courtesy National Archives and Records Administration.*

Other diversions involved a visit by the regimental commander, Colonel Zenas Bliss, who traveled from Fort Bayard, New Mexico, to inspect elements of his dispersed command. Probably more to the liking of the soldiers, dances took place, one of which Fort Huachuca's veterans organization, Army and Navy Union Garrison No. 66, sponsored on July 4, 1893. Reportedly, this "grand ball" drew a large crowd who enjoyed the music furnished by the string band of Company B, Twenty-Fourth Infantry. Notably, this improvised musicians' group stood in for the regimental band, which served at Fort Bayard. In this regard, the Twenty-Fourth was the only one of the Buffalo Soldier units not to have their bandsmen on duty in Arizona.

Regardless of the source of music, these soirees required dance partners. During the first years of the regiment's existence, single soldiers dominated. By the 1890s, however, that situation had changed. Indeed, by the time the Twenty-Fourth garrisoned Fort Huachuca, it ranked among the ten regiments with the most married men (sixty-one) and spouses (forty) in a garrison.

One of the members of the Twenty-Fourth Infantry, in this instance posted to Fort Bowie, Arizona, began married life in an unusual manner. According to the *Arizona Republican* of June 16, 1892, Chaplain B.C. Hammond, who officiated, did so from Fort Apache, situated hundreds of miles to the north. The couple, Corporal James A. Hardee, Company C, Twenty-Fourth Infantry, and Miss Hattie Quinn of St. Louis, Missouri, exchanged their vows via telegraph, with the chaplain posing the usual questions. At the ceremony's end, he pronounced them "man and wife."

EDUCATION AND REGIMENTAL CHAPLAINS

Technology aside, more than a dozen years after the entry of Black regulars into the U.S. Army, illiteracy remained a challenge. Beginning with the Civil War, the Union War Department authorized regimental chaplains for the units of the U.S. Colored Troops. These military men of the cloth attended to spiritual matters as well as developed programs to assist Black soldiers, many of whom previously had been enslaved and were denied opportunities to obtain even the most rudimentary schooling.

Immediately after the Civil War, many Black and white U.S. Army soldiers still lacked the ability to read or write. The 1866 Congressional legislation that established the Black regiments provided one advantage not offered to the white rank and file. These six units would be assigned regimental chaplains rather than the standard practice, through 1901, of all other military clergymen being assigned to garrisons as post chaplains. Nonetheless, it was not until 1889 that the military mandated that all personnel without an elementary education must attend school. By 1892, between nine and fifteen men from the Twenty-Fourth spent part of their day in class.

Originally, white chaplains oversaw instruction in the Black regiments. Then, in 1884, the War Department allowed the first Black chaplain, Henry V. Plummer, to serve with the Ninth Cavalry. Over the next three score years and more, Reverend Plummer would be followed by no fewer that ten other "sky pilots," as military chaplains came to be known colloquially. Between 1886 and 1939, the role of honor included a diverse, impressive group of clergymen, most of whom spent part of their military career in Arizona. Each of them embodied W.E.B. Du Bois's concept of the "Talented Tenth," an extraordinary group of Black soldiers who achieved inspiring goals:

- Theophilus G. Steward
- George W. Prioleau, retired on May 14, 1920, age sixty-four
- William T. Anderson
- Washington E. Gladden
- O.J.W. Scott
- Louis A. Carter
- Alexander W. Thomas
- Monroe S. Caver
- Isaac C. Snowden

Although not stationed in Arizona, the first Black military clergyman to perform his dual duties in the Southwest was Allen Allensworth. Like Henry Plummer, he had been enslaved before the Civil War. Fearlessly, he escaped from his bondage and fled north. For a time, he served with the Illinois Volunteers and assisted with hospital work. Eventually, he joined the U.S. Navy. By war's end, he had become a petty officer. In 1885, after completing higher education and ministering to a civilian congregation, he successfully secured the chaplaincy of the Twenty-Fourth Infantry. By the early 1890s, he was serving mainly at Fort Bayard, New Mexico, but his influence extended to members of the regiment stationed in Arizona. A staunch champion of education, he particularly advocated for vocational training not unlike his contemporary, Booker T. Washington. To this end, he published a manual detailing a system of progressive education. Furthermore, he urged Black candidates to seek appointments to the U.S. Military Academy.

In 1893, the well-traveled clergyman even reported to the World Columbian Exposition in Chicago on special assignment from this regiment. While there, he delivered a lecture titled "Life in a Military Garrison," a synopsis of which appeared in the *Chicago Tribune*. According to the newspaper, among Allensworth's statements, he spoke of how the profits derived from the sale of beer and other articles were given to the soldiers to purchase luxuries for their tables. An education akin the common English branches was given the soldier so that when he returned to civilian life, he would be prepared for "intelligent citizenship." Adding to the positive picture painted by Allensworth, he described the soldier's social life as "cosmopolitan in

For two decades, Chaplain Allen Allensworth ministered to his soldier congregation from the Twenty-Fourth Infantry. *Courtesy the author.*

character and each endeavored to make life pleasant for the others." He added, "The false impression has prevailed among a large class of civilians as to the character and composition of the United States army....Among its officers were to be found noble men of honor and culture, and among their families, women of education, refinement, and Christian graces. Among the enlisted men, education, excellent character, and laudable ambition were common, and the rank and file of a military garrison would compare favorably with any community of the same number of inhabitants."

Those chaplains who followed Reverend Allensworth not only echoed positive views about their soldier flocks, but they also continued to promote educational opportunities for the rank and file. In many ways, their perspectives bore out, but this was not always the case.

DIVERGENCE FROM DUTY

As evidence, according to a December 24, 1892 reference in the *Army and Navy Journal*, "Captain Edgar S. Dudley, Acting Judge Advocate, Department of Arizona, in his annual report states the number of trials of enlisted men by Court-martial in that department, and says: 'The regiment having the largest number tried is the 24th Infantry.'" Some officers opined, whether true or not, that "the general character of the colored soldier for sobriety is deteriorating." Adding some substance to this contention, in 1892, after standing general courts-martial, some sixteen members of the regiment received dishonorable discharges. Even supposedly stalwart Sergeant Benjamin Brown, reputably one of the best marksmen in the army, fell from grace from time to time. Fort Huachuca's commanding officer, Lieutenant Colonel Henry V. Noyes of the Second Cavalry, twice cited the NCO for misbehavior. For the first infraction, Noyes rescinded Brown's furlough "because he loafed around post most of the time since 1 Nov 1892."

More seriously, by the spring of 1893, Brown had "stopped at a house of ill fame on the north border of the reservation." While there, "John Riley [aka Reilly], proprietor of a brothel just off the reservation at Fort Huachuca," killed another enlisted man from Company C, thirty-five-year-old Private Jim Easly. Riley pled self-defense. Just a few days later, testimony led to Riley's discharge from custody.

A satirical statement about Riley's establishment (known in the slang of the era as a "hog ranch") appeared in the December 24, 1893 issue of the *Tombstone Epitaph*. The editor sardonically remarked:

> *The proposition to cut down the military reservations of the country to five thousand acres each is a more in the right direction. There are a great many reasons why it should be done. This will not only throw open a large extent of valuable mineral and agricultural land to settlement, but will be a great boon to the soldiers, who are now compelled to travel four or five miles to reach a hog ranch.*
>
> *These apparently necessary evils can under the new law move under the shadow of the canteen and quench the thirst of our flag's defenders without compelling them to walk ten miles after dark.*

Earlier in the year, the same newspaper for February 1, 1893, carried an equally ironical nod to the unsavory appendage to the post. Supposedly, "a traveler going north yesterday morning was inquiring where Hog ranch is. As no such place is mentioned on the map of Arizona, we conclude be must be going to the suburbs of Ft. Huachuca." Of course, this was not the only garrison to have the dubious distinction of having a hog ranch nearby. For example, on the outskirts of Fort Bowie, a brothel and bar did "a good business in selling whisky," especially to the Apache soldiers stationed there who had enlisted as infantrymen during a short-lived experiment to convert Native Americans into army enlisted men. On April 6, 1893, the *St. Johns*

Herald carried a warning couched in racist overtones: "Unless this business is stopped there will be serious trouble. The Apaches are irresponsible beings when sober and hopelessly insane when intoxicated. The ranchers and miners in the vicinity of Bowie's 'Hog Ranch' are fearful of an outbreak at any time, and the responsibility for trouble when it occurs will rest between conscienceless individuals who sell the liquor and the government which seems powerless to stop it."

An African American couple, probably servants to the officers and their families, enjoy a picnic outing near Fort Bowie not long before the post was abandoned during the early 1890s. *Courtesy the author.*

While this prediction evidently did not come to pass, a violent episode occurred during October 1893. Once again, a shooting took place at John Reilley's Star Ranch and ended when another private from the Twenty-Fourth, named Robinson, fatally shot a comrade named West. Robinson fled. A pair of Indian scouts and two officers from Fort Huachuca vowed to capture him but failed. Instead, Robinson voluntarily gave himself up at the post after lack of food compelled him to surrender. A preliminary hearing produced mixed versions of the altercations. Among those who testified was Ellen Reilly, John Reilly's spouse, who supported Robinson's claim of self-defense, as did none other than Sergeant Benjamin Brown and two fellow Company C men, Corporal Thornton Jackson and Private Alonzo Warnzer, all of whom painted West as a quarrelsome drunkard and Robinson as an individual of good character who acted in a manner that the defense witnesses would have taken if faced with a similar threat.

On November 29, 1893, Robinson stood before the bench, charged with manslaughter. Testimony in his favor disposed "the necessity of the jury retiring. The witnesses failed to show that Robinson had acted otherwise than in a justifiable manner in killing his assailant," as Tombstone's *Arizona Kicker* reported. Subsequently, the judge afterward "instructed the jury to find a verdict of not guilty, which was done in open court."

NONCOMMISSIONED OFFICERS AND ENLISTED MEN

At times, Brown and some compatriots from his company were far from model enlisted men. In 1892, among other things, upward of twenty-four members of the company went absent without leave. Brown's lack of decorum may have contributed to this situation. Be that as it may, Sergeant Brown rose to the rank of regimental sergeant major when his predecessor obtained a promotion to post ordnance sergeant. However, in 1898, demons again plagued Brown. He was reduced in rank from the top position of regimental sergeant major to the lowest rung as a private. Later that year, he earned back two stripes as a corporal. By 1903, he had regained status by becoming the regiment's drum major.

One of Brown's predecessors as the sergeant major of the Twenty-Fourth, George Lewis, also surrendered his chevrons as the regiment's senior NCO to become a corporal in Troop I, Ninth Cavalry. After forging checks and deserting, Lewis, who had "the reputation being a smart individual," nonetheless was arrested, sent to the guardhouse, tried and found guilty.

Fortunately, former sergeants Major Brown and Lewis represented exceptions to the otherwise usually enviable record of soldiers in the

Twenty-Fourth Infantry. In fact, Lewis especially diverged from the norm in a significant respect. Desertion, often the scourge of the frontier army, occurred far less often among Black regulars, as underscored in the secretary of war's 1889 annual report. While white regiments averaged a 12 percent desertion rate, Black regiments lost only 2 percent of their strength that year. As other evidence, in 1892, only four men deserted from the Twenty-Fourth Infantry, singling them out as the best unit in the U.S. Army. Two years later, only two soldiers disappeared from Fort Huachuca. The other daunting evil of the army in the West, excessive alcohol consumption, tended to be less a problem for Black personnel. Once more, a summation in the secretary of war's report for July 1, 1890–June 30, 1891 offered telling statistics:

> *Drunkenness is on the decrease among our troops. The average annual rate per thousand of strength during the decade 1879–1889 was, among the white men, 62.22; during 1889, it was 45.64; and during 1890, 44.45. The colored soldier is seldom on sick report from this cause; his average annual rate during the decade was 4.42, the rate of last year was 2.07, and of the present year 5.59.*

A third strength of the Black regiments appeared in the high rates of reenlistment found among African American regiments in contrast to whites. As a case in point, in 1893, the secretary of war concluded that the long service of soldiers in Twenty-Fourth stood in the top echelons of the army. Furthermore, the regiment boasted nineteen noncommissioned officers who had served for twenty years or more, a statistic only surpassed by fellow Black units and one white regiment, the Second Artillery. Additionally, at the same time, 28 privates from the Twenty-Fourth had more than twenty years in uniform, equaled only by the white soldiers in the Nineteenth Infantry and outdone by one white unit, the Fourth Artillery, with an impressive total of 29. Finally, 124 soldiers from the Twenty-Fourth each claimed more than five years in the ranks, this being the highest number of enlisted men in the same regiment. These numbers took on more meaning in that the strengths of regiments during this period typically amounted to about 600 enlisted men per regiment.

According to Steven Smith's *The African American Soldier at Fort Huachuca*, all these factors

> *probably contributed greatly to morale and low incidences of desertion and crime. The above record points to a regiment composed of men with long*

service records, who knew each other well, and were loyal to their regiment. Certainly the record was partially due to the lack of opportunities for African Americans outside the Army. Getting a job was difficult for blacks and actually developing a career was almost unheard-of. The Army offered a career, housing, clothing and food. But service in the Army was also a source of pride within the African American community. Civilian whites looked down on soldiers regardless of race—African Americans did not. This helped build pride among African American soldiers as being part of something important within their own race.

COMRADES AND COMMUNITY BUILDERS

One unique aspect of the Black military experience in Arizona bespoke of the camaraderie that could develop among long-serving soldiers. Friendships might endure beyond time in the army. This especially existed at a post-military haven: Allensworth, California. Named for its most notable founder, Twenty-Fourth Infantry chaplain Allen Allensworth, the settlement located south of Hanford in Tulare County emerged in the early twentieth century. This self-contained community—complete with a school, church, mercantile and other trappings of a small town—served the needs of its agriculturally based citizenship.

Reverend Allensworth specifically sought out soldiers and their families, whom early residents referred to as "the Sergeants." This quest for former military men came about for many, varied reasons. Elizabeth Payne McGhee, whose father, William Payne, was an early resident, shared one motive born of a reaction to widespread racial prejudice of the era. She revealed, "Since so many ex-soldiers were there, they formed protective groups. They even went so far as to drill, and they had signals so if anything happened in the town and we had to get together for protection, they had signals they'd give, and people a mile and a half away would get together. They trained and got real good, but they never once said anything about the little town—but they were ready." McGhee added two other salient details. One of the most important facts she offered disclosed that several of these veterans formerly served at Fort Huachuca. Besides being dependable, their pensions provided "money, to build and buy farm equipment."

Indeed, most of the experienced noncommissioned officers had spent years together in the Twenty-Fourth Infantry. The roster included Sergeants

Joseph Brown, Thomas Hamlin, George Hixon, Robert Howard, William Jenkins, Joseph Lee and John Taylor. Then there was Sergeant George Carver, formerly of Company E, Twenty-Fourth Infantry, who ranked fifty-second among expert riflemen in the army during 1904. Now he exchanged a rifle for a glove as the first baseman on the town's ball team. Another man, named Nash, must have had a more than passing knowledge of firearms because he managed the gun club for wealthy whites a number of miles to the south of the colony.

William Fox of Company B, Twenty-Fourth Infantry, was reduced from sergeant to private while in Company D and fined thirty dollars for threatening his first sergeant and assaulting a corporal. As an unassigned recruit at Fort Bayard, he came down on a levy under Order 246 on December 19, 1893, along with three other privates bound for Fort Huachuca. Evidently, Fox eventually mended his ways sufficiently to be accepted by Chaplain Allensworth for the colony.

James Phillips enlisted in Chicago on August 14, 1893. He first joined Fox with Company B at Fort Huachuca. Phillips later went to Company H. He saw action in Cuba during 1898 and then received his discharge with an "excellent" character reference. Later that year, on September 26, Phillips reenlisted at Fort Douglas, Utah. It was there that he served as a special duty laborer in the subsistence department beginning on October 2, 1898. By 1905, as a private with Company M, he had obtained recognition as a marksman. At Allensworth, he and his family lived in a prefabricated house that locals assisted in erecting. This structure stood just behind Chaplain Allensworth's home. Phillips died in San Francisco. At that time, the chaplain's daughter, Josephine Allensworth, along with "Sarah Hindsman, Cora Overr, Sarah Porter (mother of Mrs. Birdie Phillips), and Laura Smith—helped Phillip's widow [Birdie] petition the Army" for her survivor's pension of twelve dollars per month. Once again, this assistance offered yet another example of cohesion often found within the military community even after leaving service.

At Fort Huachuca, Phillips served alongside John R. Green, a sergeant in Company A. While at Fort Apache, Private Green met Chaplain Allensworth. After Green transferred to Fort Bayard, New Mexico, the clergyman had him appointed as the post schoolteacher. Later, Green taught at Fort Huachuca. In another telling point about Green, while at Fort Huachuca, he and his wife each donated one dollar to the defense fund for three Black women charged with murder in Lunenburg County, Virginia. Fellow Company A sergeant Frank Banks and his wife matched the Greens in this effort. Green, who signed the letter with the accompanying donation, remarked, "While we earnestly believe the women to be innocent, the murder was committed by some one, and this alone is enough to inspire every Afro-American to do all in their power to clear the innocent and let the guilty be punished."

Yet another sergeant, James "Bunky" Grimes from the Twenty-Fourth Infantry, who had been wounded in Cuba, retired to Allensworth. He acquired an impressive eleven and a half acres. Similarly, the Twenty-Fourth's Sergeant G.W. Hicks held three city lots and a ten-acre ranch in alfalfa. For the most part, the Allensworth military pioneers fared well after leaving the military. They constituted a fortunate few. Often, veterans from the half century after the Civil War faced financial hardship.

Another common denominator for the Allensworth veterans related to their posting in 1896 to Fort Douglas, Utah. Two years after, the regiment entrained for Georgia, where they readied themselves for their first overseas assignment in Cuba as a significant element of the invasion force dispatched there during the Spanish-American War. Along with the other three regiments of Black regulars, they acquitted themselves honorably in combat. When the fighting ceased, they unselfishly volunteered to aid the sick and wounded. In the process, thirty-one of them died most likely from yellow fever.

All these experiences came about after the late 1893 transfer from Arizona. Except for periodic travel of the Twenty-Fourth's baseball and football teams and some of their formidable boxers, the regiment seldom was present at their former postings.

FINAL DAYS IN ARIZONA

There were some exceptions, however, including a tragic one that took place in Nogales during late May 1919. While on furlough from the Twenty-Fourth's main duty station at that time, Company G's First Sergeant Wilbur Earl returned to Nogales, where he and his spouse had a home. After his return, he killed her in their residence and then committed suicide. According to an investigation that followed, he did so out of jealousy, although no details emerged in the aftermath of this tragedy.

In fact, as Nogales's *Border Vidette* noted on September 15, 1917, that the first "battalion of the famous 24th Infantry…arrived here last Sunday from Columbus, New Mexico, and went into camp on the site formerly

The Twenty-Fourth Infantry's distinctive unit insignia, originally approved on January 12, 1923, and amended on March 21, 1923, consisted of a gold color metal and enamel device with a blue disc bearing a white blockhouse, with tower masoned and roofed in gold below a gold scroll inscribed "San Juan" in blue letters. Below the disc appeared a gold scroll turned blue and inscribed with the regimental motto, "Semper Paratus," in blue letters. The fortifications commemorate the regiment's 1898 assault on San Juan Santiago de Cuba. *Courtesy the author.*

occupied by the Idaho troops, near the cemetery. There are fifteen officers and about eight hundred men." One week later, many of them participated in the opening of the camp's YMCA. Highlights of the program included a prayer from the acting regimental chaplain, a piano solo from a member of Company B and a performance by a male quartet from the same company. Private Reed from Company D and Private Ferguson of Troop C, Tenth Cavalry, performed a clog dance, followed by a piano and violin duet offered by two men from Company B. At the same time, the second battalion took up temporary duty at Douglas.

Moreover, a battalion transferred to Naco, where it relieved national guardsmen from the First Arizona Infantry. According to the *Bisbee Daily Review* for October 14, 1917, they "had been there for a number of months."

Once in place, they assumed traditional responsibilities as border guards at the customs house. A few weeks passed before some of the first Black draftees to be called up for service in World War I arrived at camp. One of the battalion's sergeants offered the draftees preliminary military instruction that likely assisted the untried inductees once they reached Camp Funston, Kansas, for basic training.

Some of the regiment's other sergeants received temporary promotions as commissioned officers, which meant they left the Twenty-Fourth for the duration of their assignments. Furthermore, during November 1917, the first and second battalions packed their kits and returned to New Mexico. This ended the regiment's days in Arizona save for an occasional journey back from New Mexico to play baseball against other Black military teams.

CHAPTER 4

TWENTY-FIFTH INFANTRY

"ONWARD"

ORIGINS

As was true for the Twenty-Fourth Infantry, the Twenty-Fifth Infantry regiment came into being as a result of the 1869 reorganization act. This legislation not only reduced the size of the U.S. Army but also consolidated the infantry regiments, which in the case of the Twenty-Fifth traced its lineage to the former Thirty-Ninth and Fortieth Infantry regiments. During April 1869, these short-lived units combined. After being reconstituted in Louisiana, the unit spread out to Texas. In due course, the regiment garrisoned posts in South Dakota, Minnesota and Montana, where among other duties they participated in the 1896–97 bicycle experiment launched from Fort Missoula. In 1898, some of these wheelmen sailed with the regiment to Cuba. Upon the Twenty-Fifth's return to the United States, it briefly served in New York, Colorado and Arizona.

In the latter case, Company A reported to Fort Huachuca from late October 1898 through April 1899. Soon the unit transferred to Fort Bliss, Texas, and remained there during the Philippine Insurrection. Company H also arrived at Fort Huachuca during October 1898. It continued to serve at that post until June, when orders assigned the company to Manila. Prior to departing for the Philippines, as John H. Nankivell summarized in *The History of the 25ᵗʰ Regiment*, "The last two months of 1898 and the early part of 1899 was a period of rehabilitation for the regiment. Officers that had been on leave or detached service rejoined the regiment, and several of the older

After the Spanish-American War, the Twenty-Fifth Infantry briefly returned to the United States. Soon thereafter, Company H received orders to leave Fort Huachuca and rendezvous with the regiment in San Francisco. The men subsequently sailed from there for the Philippines. *Courtesy United States Army Heritage and Education Center.*

enlisted men that had been absent, sick or on detached service also rejoined. Recruits were being received in large drafts and the clothing, equipping, and training, of these men entailed a vast amount of work."

AFTER ARIZONA

Following this short-lived respite, the Twenty-Fifth sailed to the Philippines. For several years, some of these infantrymen encountered intense Filipino opposition to the United States' occupation of the islands. In 1902, after this daunting duty, the Twenty-Fifth sailed home to perform garrison duty at various posts in the western United States. This included one battalion being sent to Brownsville, Texas, where in 1906, running afoul of local authorities and prejudicial Jim Crow laws, violence broke out that led to the dismissal of nearly all of the enlisted men in the battalion.

In the wake of this incident, with many replacements filling the ranks for the dubiously discharged men, the Twenty-Fifth headed back to the Philippines. After that, more stateside tours followed at such diverse stations as the state of Washington and eventually Hawaii from 1913 to 1918. Thus, during World War I, the regiment saw no action in Europe.

RETURN TO THE BORDER

Then, in 1918, the Twenty-Fifth transferred to Arizona, at first mainly to Camp Stephen D. Little. It arrived a few days after the Battle at Ambos Nogales. Although the regiment escaped combat, during its long years on the border, the Twenty-Fifth remained in readiness to respond to a future threat. Fortunately, it never had to take up arms on the border. Indeed, during the Twenty-Fifth's stay in the borderlands, it served peacefully in Nogales, Ajo, Yuma and other Arizona locations, as well as occasionally in Andrade, California. Over the course of nearly a quarter of a century in the state, the regiment also generally enjoyed quiet relations with the civilian populace of Arizona and with the residents south of the line in Sonora.

PHILANTHROPY

These exchanges tended to be positive and based on Black military personnel's regular participation in patriotic celebrations, religious ceremonies, concerts and an array of musical performances by the regimental band along with various talented members of the rank and file.

While on duty in Yuma, a contingent from the Twenty-Fifth Infantry set aside their military assignments to hold a party. *Courtesy the author.*

Further, they added to the social fabric of Arizona communities such as Yuma, where the *Phoenix Tribune* for September 21, 1918, touted a "BRILLIANT SOCIAL FUNCTION" held earlier in the month in the city's auditorium. The dance, sponsored by Company B, Twenty-Fifth Infantry, afforded an "opportunity for the city to turn out in full and really show what everybody thinks of Uncle Sam's boys." Also of significance, the paper remarked, "The outstanding feature of this affair was the wonderful attendance by all nationalities. The Colored soldiers deported themselves in such a manner as would reflect credit upon their noble calling. Sergeant Jenkins reported $50.00 given to the Red Cross as the results of the dance."

This was not the only time the Black military members donated money from their rather meager pay. In January 1920, for instance, both officers and men from the Twenty-Fifth Infantry made "generous contributions to victims of earthquake in Vera Cruz and Puebla, Mexico," as the *Daily Morning Oasis* in Nogales, Arizona, mentioned both on January 30, 1920, and January 31, 1920. Later that year, they once more demonstrated their willingness to help with monetary contributions. This time, they gave to another cause, Tucson's Arizona Children's Home. Of the $1,535 pledged

A no-nonsense Twenty-Fifth Infantry private strikes a pose in his ready-for-action field uniform. All that is missing is his Springfield M 1903 rifle and web gear for him to respond to the call to arms. *Courtesy University of Arizona Library Special Collections.*

by residents of Nogales, approximately $80 came from the Twenty-Fifth Infantry at Camp Little.

In November 1925, the Tenth Cavalry at Fort Huachuca and the various contingents of the Twenty-Fifth Infantry "went over the top in raising funds for the worthy Red Cross organization," or so stated Nogales, Arizona's *International*. The next month, the same paper noted that the local Kiwanis held the biggest Christmas Day event in town by distributing gifts to those in need. Some three thousand from Ambos Nogales, Sonora, received presents given out from the seasonal symbolic Yule tree in front of the city hall. Traffic backed up, requiring a diversion of vehicles to other streets while the many recipients collected food, clothing and other items. Adding to the festivities, the Twenty-Fifth Infantry Band entertained with one of the many concerts it presented during its long stay in the twin border towns.

MUSIC, LOTS OF MUSIC

As often noted in the *Daily Morning Oasis* and its counterpart, the *International*, free public concerts in Nogales, Arizona, entertained any and all. Impressive programs, especially under the able baton of the regimental bandleader Leslie King, offered a varied repertoire, ranging from classical excerpts to popular tunes of the time. Once more, as incongruous as it appears to later audiences, local military sponsors even booked minstrel shows such as the one that opened in Nogales's Lyric Theater during February 1920. The *Daily Oasis* touted Washburn's Minstrels as "one of the merriest, danciest and jazziest group of artists ever assembled. You positively must not miss the Big Jazz Band Concert and grand Street Parade."

The Washburn's Minstrels event took place at the Lyric perhaps because the Nogales Theater had suffered a fire during the previous month. The crowd of Black soldiers and civilians fled without any casualties.

By the late 1920s, vaudeville had been added to the entertainment seen, although the audience numbered fewer than one hundred. A smallpox scare kept the audience small. The variety show included a magic act, singing, dancing, a corps of comedians, some athletic performances, the tossing of flaming clubs and music. The performance of the Camp Jones quartet in particular prompted applause.

Besides availing themselves of entertainment, there were times when soldiers from the Twenty-Fifth participated in more somber observances.

As one example, during the summer of 1921, after the popular young Nogales businessmen George Arthur Sullivan died, a contingent of the regiment took part in the funeral. As the *Border Vidette* of July 16, 1921, indicated, "The Twenty-Fifth Infantry band, from Camp Stephen D. Little" played a funeral dirge as it "led the procession from the undertaking parlors to the train this afternoon. Following the band came a firing squad from the Twenty fifth Infantry, the hearse, pallbearers, flag bearers carrying the United States and American Legion flags, and delegations of American Legion and Knights of Columbus, and friends." Closer to home, all four Buffalo Soldier regiments, including the Twenty-Fifth Infantry, conducted solemn memorial services in recognition of the passing of Colonel Charles Young.

Many years after the fact, in the March 9, 1945 *Apache Sentinel*, Staff Sergeant Joseph H. Gaillard reminisced that John Philip Sousa once rated the Twenty-Fifth Infantry Band "as one of the best Army bands in the country." He also recalled that "its director, first M/Sgt., then Lieutenant King, was its leader," a musician on whom he likewise bestowed the "title of 'gentleman,' which to him means much."

ATHLETICS

By the time the Twenty-Fifth took up station at Nogales, football had begun to make inroads. As one example, at the end of 1919, the regiment's team left for Fort Huachuca, where they bested the Tenth Cavalry on the gridiron by a score of 19–7. A few months earlier, the *Daily Morning Oasis* of October 29, 1919, remarked that the "Soldiers of the 25th infantry were out yesterday afternoon in football uniform. They have a splendid team and they surely do know how to carry that old football."

On Armistice Day (Memorial Day), held on November 11, 1926, the American Legion hosted a program that included a morning parade in which both the Twenty-Fifth Infantry and Tenth Cavalry participated alongside Mexican troops, five bands, floats, civilian organizations and schoolchildren. In the afternoon, a football game preceded a rather unusual element: a military gymkhana. That night, the Twenty-Fifth Infantry's band provided music at a grand ball at the high school gymnasium. To attract guests from Sonora, all passport regulations were waived on the border on the day of the celebration.

Track and field meets, both as intra- and inter-regimental events, kept the soldiers fit, provided a break from routine and offered yet another opportunity for soldiers and civilians to congregate, as Douglas's *Daily Dispatch* for March 26, 1928, relayed about a matchup of the regiment's first battalion who competed at Camp Jones. For the most part, the standard events dominated, but some military-specific events added to the program. The equipment race—which involved donning their field gear, sprinting toward a goal, shelter tent pitching and disassembly, along with grenade throwing—provided diverse means to demonstrate martial capabilities.

Other athletes from the Twenty-Fifth climbed into the ring. Early on, "smokers," reported the *Daily Morning Oasis* on November 11, 1919, could be a "howling success, as usual. An enthusiastic crowd of the sporting fraternity of Nogales was present, amongst them quite a number of ladies, and by the pleased expressions upon the faces of all one could tell they enjoyed every minute of the attraction." Lightweights, middleweights, welterweights and heavyweights all could be found on varied programs, some of which were presented at Camp Little's Ali Baba Theater, a spacious facility completed under the supervision of Quartermaster Sergeant Charles Mingus Sr.

Mingus first enlisted at Richmond, Virginia. Then he reported to the Tenth Cavalry. By March 14, 1897, he had advanced to corporal in Troop G of the regiment. After a brief stint as a civilian, he reenlisted in the army. This time he went to the Twenty-Fourth Infantry. After that, he traveled widely, eventually being sent to Nogales's Camp Little.

His long military career ended in Nogales on a high note reflective of the larger Buffalo Soldier heritage in Arizona. In 1920, he earned his commanding officer's praise for successful completion of the Camp Little's first movie theater. The December 20, 1920 *Nogales Daily Oasis* recognized that the sergeant took "charge of the work, superintended it and prosecuted it to a conclusion."

Periodically, boxers from the Twenty-Fifth traveled to Fort Huachuca and sparred with opponents from the Tenth Cavalry. While at the fort, during the summer of 1926, they took part in the Tenth's organization day commemorations along with a large number of visitors from neighboring towns who drove in for the festive show. As part of the festivities, they could enjoy a barbecue supper. From time to time, pugilists from the Twenty-Fifth traveled to Nogales, Sonora's bull ring for open-air expositions. As with other units, track and field events drew spectators and kept many men physically fit.

Members of the Twenty-Fifth Infantry track team competed against fellow infantrymen from their regiment, as well as against opponents from the Tenth Cavalry. *Courtesy University of Arizona Library Special Collections.*

Nonetheless, the *Douglas Daily Dispatch*'s conclusion on June 19, 1927, rang true: "Everyone likes to see a negro play baseball or fight on a boxing card. It would seem, that this Camp Little baseball team would pack 'em in. These boys play real ball and always furnish plenty of comedy."

MORE THAN A GAME

Certainly, the major force that helped enhance community relations took place on the diamond. Baseball remained the most popular sport among these enlisted men, these Buffalo Soldiers. From the late nineteenth century through World War II, Black enlisted men enjoyed the national pastime both

Left: Charles Wilber "Bullet Joe" Rogan, who served variously in the Twenty-Fourth and Twenty-Fifth Infantry, played baseball with the "Wreckers" of the latter regiment. His dual talents as a pitcher and outfielder led him to a career in the sport, starring with the Kansas City Monarchs of the Negro Baseball Leagues. *Courtesy Fort Huachuca Museum.*

Right: An unidentified member of the Twenty-Fifth Infantry's legendary "Wreckers" baseball team sports a team sweater. *Courtesy University of Arizona Library Special Collections.*

as participants and as spectators. They avidly watched the games and followed seasons closely. In so doing, they witnessed many incredible plays and players. In the latter instance, as James Finley underscored in his fine multipart series on the Black military experience at Fort Huachuca, the spectators saw firsthand that "some of the best men…[were] recruited into the Negro Leagues." Indeed, at least a half dozen of the roster later signed with the storied Kansas City Monarchs: Oscar "Heavy" Johnson, Lem Hawkins, Bob Fagan, Walter "Dobie" Moore, Hurly McNair and Wilbur Rogan. The last named exceptionally multitalented player eventually acquired the nickname "Bullet Joe." During his days with the military, however, Jerry Malloy stated in the National Pastime that Rogan received the sobriquet "Cap" because, in the words of one veteran of the Twenty-Fifth, "in the army at that time a Captain was somebody and on the ball field Cap Rogan was somebody." At the same time, Moore, known for his huge hands, stood out as a "great hitter, base runner, and a sensational shortstop."

Rogan played alongside Dobie Moore, Hurly McNair, Oscar "Heavy" Johnson, Lem Hawkins and Bob Fagan. This lineup later played with the storied Kansas City Monarchs, arguably the most celebrated team of the bygone Negro Leagues. Before leaving the ranks for professional careers, they had gained the apt nickname "the Wreckers." Certainly, they wreaked havoc on much of the opposition. By the time the Wreckers reached Nogales, Arizona, they had been in existence in one form or another since being established in the early 1890s. The original members and those who followed took the game seriously, as did their fellow Black foot soldiers, who displayed pride in their team. Beyond being fine athletes, the Wreckers drew people together who previously may have been strangers or even enemies. That was so in Hawaii, when the regiment served before and during World War I.

The tradition, established by the fine athletes of the days when the Wreckers ruled, continued into the 1930s. As Bisbee's *Brewery Gulch Gazette* for June 22, 1934, reported, "That Fort Huachuca baseball team is just about the 4 best aggregation of ball tossers that the post has turned out in the last few years. It reminds us of that team that was with either the 24th or 25th infantry about ten years ago on which played the famous Rogan, afterward with the Kansas City Monarchs. Several others of those colored soldiers afterward played in the Negro professional league of which the Monarch team was a member."

Previously, the Twenty-Fifth's ballplayers gained status in Nogales and elsewhere in southern Arizona. As the April 19, 1919 issue of Nogales's *Border Vidette* rightly reported, "The baseball team of the 25th Infantry now stationed here is one of the best in the Army." Little wonder then that, early on, these kings of swat crossed bats with the likes of the "crack Douglas team" as they faced off in "two mighty fast, interesting games."

Several months later, on October 29, 1919, the paper announced another faceoff "between 25th Infantry Wreckers and All Stars from Kansas City." The Wreckers were about to do battle with a young barnstormer, Casey Stengel (later the New York Yankees legendary manager) and his All-Stars. This was a composite corps of off-season pros put together by Stengel of "major and minor league stars." Always looking for an opposing team, he sought to play the Twenty-Fifth's nine in Nogales. As a result, the regimental athletic officer received a telegram "from Stengle's [*sic*] all star aggregation of Kansas City, Mo., trying to arrange three games." An *Oasis* reporter then challenged, "It is now up to sport fans and fanettes to make these games a success" by buying tickets at fifty cents each.

The October 30 edition of the *Oasis* predicted, "More diamond fame is expected by the 25th infantry baseball stars in the games to be played Monday, Tuesday and Wednesday of next week with Casey Stengle's [*sic*] All Stars" when the army nine played the visitors "at the Athletic Field, east of Morley avenue and the Patagonia road." The paper based its positive prophecy on the strength that "[t]he cream of the 25th infantry players has been skimmed to represent Nogales, and a good game is anticipated." In readiness, the Black ballplayers took to "the field of battle" where they resolutely practiced for the much-publicized events.

Would these prognostications come true, or were they idle boasts about the local favorites? The answer soon came in rapid succession. The Wreckers stepped up on November 3 to win the first engagement of the three game series 5–4. The *Daily Morning Oasis* anticipated "A CLOSE GAME" characterized by "SOME SENSATIONAL PLAYING."

The initial win was no walk off, as revealed in the recap by the *Oasis*. "Right at the start," shared the reporter, "in the first inning, the visitors knocked off a score of four runs, which made things look blue for the Wreckers, but that was all they got. After that they won only a succession of goose eggs." As the innings mounted, "in the third…the Wreckers pulled off a couple of runs and repeated the dose in the fifth, and in the seventh they took the one run needed to make the game." None other than Moore, who might be dubbed the MVP, took a mighty swing "with the willow." The batter "landed on the flying sphere just right, and it just kept climbing into the air until when it began to come down it was away over in the vicinity of Yaqui village, and before it had been recovered Moore had made the circle of the bases, coming safe to the home plate." An enthusiastic crowd witnessed this stirring baseball game, as well as also took pleasure in "the music played by the Twenty-Fifth Infantry band and the buglers, which seemed to give the Wreckers fresh courage and the All Stars the blues," or so the *Oasis* sportswriter concluded.

The November 4 slugfest proved another crowd pleaser, with "a great amount of pep displayed on both sides." In the beginning, "the Wreckers made good" with their leadoff batter, who slammed a home run followed by another player scoring when mighty Moore drove his teammate in for another notch. All appeared as if a repeat of the opening game was in the offing "until the fourth inning, when the fates seemed against the 25th; the game was the All Stars' until the end," as they demonstrated some "clever pitching." In fact, by the conclusion of "the seventh inning the All Stars were eight runs to the Wreckers' five. In the eighth inning, the All Stars made six runs and the Wreckers scored the same, both teams doing fast work. Moore of the Twenty-Fifth knocked a home run with three men on bases." Despite this impressive grand slam, the All-Stars walked away with the win.

With the teams tied for honors, on November 6, 1919, the crowd gathered for the third and final stand. At the outset, it appeared that the Wreckers would be bested again. Reacting, by the second inning, their manager changed the lineup. Even so, "The fans had given up victory to the All Stars until the fifth inning when the Wreckers woke up and played real ball....A more contented crowd witnessed the third game....The Wreckers won by a score of 8 to 6."

Little wonder then that the *Daily Morning Oasis* crowned the Wreckers as "the best team in the U.S. army" whether standing against foes from other regiments such as the segregated Black Twenty-Fourth Infantry comrades and their fellow Tenth Cavalry Buffalo Soldiers or civilian teams variously composed of whites and often with teams of combined gringo and Latino opponents as well—a stirring story for baseball in Nogales and southern Arizona long before integration, which waited until after World War II. It was not until the late 1940s that the major leagues began to relinquish decades of discrimination with Jackie Robinson's debut.

Rather than being irate, Stengel seemingly admired the Wreckers. He even stated, "They were as good as any major-leaguers." This perspective, recorded by Stengel's biographer, Robert W. Creamer, may have been the basis for him sharing his perspective with a fellow Kansas City resident. Stengel informed J.L. Wilkinson, who was in the process of forming the Monarchs, that some impressive Black talent could be found on the border. Intelligence obtained from Stengel may well have led to the recruiting of many Wreckers, whom Wilkinson enticed to exchange their U.S. Army olive drab for another type of uniform.

Even though several core members of the Wreckers would depart for the Negro Leagues, many Arizonans watched them from the stands with considerable enjoyment and perhaps more than a little admiration. Regardless of the roster, players from Twenty-Fifth Infantry—and, for that matter, the Tenth Cavalry—found a place in schedules around the state, such as appearing in Douglas, where in 1928 they constituted one of the clubs to compete in the area league.

In that year, the *Douglas Daily Dispatch* for March 7, 1928 indicated that "the first battalion team from Camp Jones which is an All-American aggregation of colored soldiers" possessed the strongest record and could be "depended on to furnish real opposition to anything which develops this year" against the other clubs, including Douglas's All-Stars. The article continued with some complex and perhaps surprising nuances:

> *The All Stars are a promising gang this year and a study of the material indicates that the army team, the Sox and the Stars are going to line up very evenly. The demand now is for a team of American young men, not of Mexican descent. It upholds the traditions of the great American game. It is pointed out that there are plenty of good ball players rusting about Douglas who have shone on high school or college teams and who could be enlisted for a real American team which could get out and offer some opposition to the Sox and the Stars and the colored boys and make some real sporting competition.*

A few weeks later, as an indication of the support that baseball elicited from fans, between three hundred and five hundred persons attended the rodeo at the fairgrounds in Douglas, while a like number turned out for two baseball games, held on separate diamonds at the same time. One of these games featured the White Sox against Company B of the Twenty-Fifth Infantry. This game was played on International Field at the south end of G Avenue. The other game took place between the Douglas All-Stars and the Company D team from Camp Jones.

An overtly biased plan for expansion envisioned at least six teams to be included with "the demand" that the clubs be composed of "far more American material in the additional teams." The prejudiced concept noted that the high school team, which was to be included, would "undoubtedly be made up of Both Americans and Mexicans. Another team is demanded which shall be made up entirely of Americans and shall be picked from older men than the high school nine to represent the American element in the battle."

MARRIAGE

Although xenophobia trumped prejudice against Black soldiers on the diamond, this dichotomy was reversed when it came to suitable marriage partners. Within the convoluted mores of the era, which championed "racial purity" and white supremacy, intermarriage between whites and nonwhites had long existed nonetheless. Just after the Civil War ended, Arizona's early territorial legislators enacted prohibitions against Blacks and mulattos from marrying whites. On December 19, 1865, the state House voted in favor of the bill with a majority of 8 to 2. When the bill went to the Council (upper house), it added "Indians and Mongolians," which was approved by a 4 to 1 margin. The law made no such distinctions for Latinos and Latinas.

Under the 1848 Treaty of Guadalupe Hidalgo, former Mexican nationals residing in the newly acquired lands released to the United States received certain rights. Allegedly, their status paralleled those enjoyed by U.S. citizens. In theory, Mexicans who remained north of the newly established border as a result of this treaty and the Gadsden Purchase in the 1850s stood on equal footing with "Caucasians." In reality, they often encountered the same bigotry experienced by other groups not deemed to be white, as indicated by the goal of the Douglas-area baseball league to be dominated by "Americans," which they defined as excluding Mexicans, especially Sonorans, and to some degree those Latinos living in the United States.

The dubious exception that classified them as "white" was intermarriage with Black citizens. On July 27, 1919, Tombstone's *Epitaph* ran a piece titled "Mexican Girl Camouflages as Yaqui to Wed Negro," which summarized this secretive practice:

> *Determined to thwart the law which prohibits the marriage of Negroes and Caucasians in this state, Maria Louisa Garcia, a comely Mexican girl of Nogales, Sonora, appeared at the manager office of County Clerk Bob Lee this morning, her face covered with shoe black in an attempt to deceive the county clerk into believing that she was a Yaqui in order that a license might be obtained to marry her sweetheart, who is a negro.*

Before then, the Santa Cruz county clerk "refused over a hundred couples marriage licenses since the Negro troops arrived here last August [1918]. Yaqui women, or women having Yaqui and Mexican blood are allowed to marry Negroes," but not Latinas. This prohibition did not dissuade Cupid. The county clerk's records indicated that over the past year, his office had issued 398 marriage licenses, of which 250 had "been secured by Negroes mostly, soldiers of the United States army." A good number of their spouses came from Honolulu, where the regiment previously served, "while quite a few have come from southern and eastern states."

Prejudicial laws in Arizona allowed Black soldiers to wed Native American women but forbade unions between Black men and Latina and white women. *Courtesy Arizona Historical Society, azB112998.*

While probably true in most cases, some soldiers circumvented restrictions or found a means to navigate the convoluted racist mores of the times. Writing many years after his wedding to the *Nogales International*, Master Sergeant Levi Biggs Sr. summarized his story as printed on March 17, 1944. His son George Washington Biggs had joined the army just as his father had done nearly three decades earlier. His father then provided a tantalizing detail. The young recruit's mother was "the former Srta. Dolores Marie Rivas, daughter of Sr. Santiago Rivas of Cananea. Son., Mexico, who is the editor of 'El Intruso.' His grandmother is Mrs. Juana H. Vasquez…a very old resident of Nogales."

The master sergeant, who reported to Nogales in 1918 with the Twenty-Fifth Infantry, considered the town his home. He and his spouse own their home in Nogales, but more to the point, it seems that the prohibition against the marriage of Black soldiers to Latinas might have been overlooked if the bride were considered a foreign national.

Not dissimilarly, after his honorable discharge on April 22, 1922, former Twenty-Fifth infantrymen Elija Gilbert "and Miss Ruby Anderson were quietly married at the bride's home." On that date, the *Phoenix Tribune* verified the nuptials. Perhaps the reason for that quiet ceremony was that the bride was "born in Old Mexico" and spoke fluent Spanish. If, as it appeared, Gilbert's spouse was of Mexican ancestry, the couple violated Arizona law.

Perhaps two other Twenty-Fifth Infantry enlisted men sought to circumvent racist nuptial barriers. The unknown Lotharios managed to induce a pair of women from Sonora to illegally cross the line and set up housekeeping with the Black infantrymen. One of them was to be a soldier's "wife while the other woman was to be 'the friend' of the second man," as a woman said in the *Daily Morning Oasis* of October 11, 1918. United States immigration service officials discovered the plan "to 'sneak' across early in the night." Instead of a happy home, they went off to jail.

The definition of "whiteness" seemed to be flexible, particularly when it involved Latinas. The one consistent baseline revolved around the concept of racial purity being maintained among whites.

Legal prohibitions did not completely deter romantic inclinations. On some occasions, matrimony, regardless of the ethnic background, took place. Some of these unions interwove civilians and soldiers together from diverse backgrounds.

RELIGION

Officiating at some of these marriages constituted but one of many duties performed by regimental chaplains. As with the other three regiments, the Twenty-Fifth Infantry boasted its share of fine military ministers. For instance, at Nogales, the garrison drew inspiration from Chaplains George Prioleau and Isaac C. Snowden. Prioleau, born five years before the outbreak of the Civil War to enslaved parents in Charleston, South Carolina, demonstrated his intellectual abilities years later. He obtained his degree in theory from Wilberforce, where he became a professor. In 1895, he received an appointment as the chaplain of the Ninth Cavalry, where he remained for two decades. Later, he transferred briefly to the Tenth Cavalry and then spent his last days in the army with the Twenty-Fifth Infantry until his 1920 retirement as a major. The next year, he was one of the founders of the Bethel AME Church in Los Angeles.

Nogales's *Daily Morning Oasis* for October 1, 1919, praised both Prioleau and his successor, Snowden, for the "increase in attendance at the religious services at the Y[MCA] building," attributing this upswing to "the influence that Chaplains Prioleau and Snowden have upon the men."

The year before, as proof of the impact of the chaplain on the regiment, Prioleau announced to his fellow civilian clergymen in Nogales "that some 2,000 men, or more, from the U.S. soldiery" in the area desired to attend the local Thanksgiving Day Union Service, or so the *Daily Morning Oasis* for November 30, 1918, printed. Good to Prioleau's word, the soldiers attended en masse the open-air Thanksgiving service, which included the regimental band and chorus. As for the offertory, civilians and soldiers alike contributed $110 for the Syrian and Armenian relief work, which was one of the many examples of soldiers donating to causes from their meager military pay.

By late November 1925, the Twenty-Fifth's chaplain, Louis Carter, was taking part in the launching of the annual Red Cross drives at Douglas and Fort Huachuca with the intention of making that year's effort as successful as the one from 1924, when both the infantrymen and cavalrymen gave generously. Reverend Carter was no stranger to such good works. In 1923, while at Camp Little, he received recognition for his fine cooperation with the Associated Charities of Nogales.

Sharing within the military community also occurred. As the *Douglas Daily Dispatch* noted on December 9, 1927, at Camp Jones, like in years past, the garrison raised up a large Christmas tree at the Service Club, which on Christmas Eve "would be piled bushels of gifts. There will be at

Chaplain George Prioleau, much like many married men in his Twenty-Fifth Infantry congregation, wed an African American woman. They thereby avoided territorial and state laws against miscegenation. *Courtesy University of Arizona Library Special Collections.*

Among the services performed by Twenty-Fifth Infantry regimental chaplains was staging holiday celebrations, which included presents and a Christmas tree at Camp Little in the 1920s. *Courtesy University of Arizona Library Special Collections.*

least one gift for every man, woman and child on the post." Several years earlier, when the regiment celebrated Christmas, the festivities included an address titled "Our Peace" delivered by Chaplain Prioleau. In the tradition of many Black minsters, Chaplain Prioleau proved an impressive orator. So, too, did his replacement, Chaplain Snowden of Tennessee. What might have been the text of one of his sermons, titled "The Spirit of the Age," appeared in the May 23, 1919 issue of the *Daily Morning Oasis*. The polished piece revealed his communication skills. Snowden, a Methodist, who received his appointment as a chaplain during World War I, seemingly shared another trait with Prioleau. Both men interacted with local clergy in Nogales in an ecumenical manner.

In another time-honored role, Chaplain Prioleau assisted with the curriculum offered at Camp Little's vocational school. As recorded in the August 3, 1919 edition of the *Bisbee Daily Review*, more than six hundred men from the Twenty-Fifth Infantry, along with troopers stationed with them from the Tenth Cavalry, displayed an interest in the program.

The chaplain oversaw the academic courses "in elementary studies" that consisted of "large classes of reading, writing and arithmetic," as well as Spanish, typewriting and bookkeeping, offering skills that permitted "the soldiers to train for non-commissioned jobs and when vacancies occur, these men will be given preference in advancement." Further, vocational opportunities were offered. Horse training, motor repair, vehicle driving lessons, blacksmithing, horse shoeing and an electrical module all were open.

PRAISE FOR THE STEADFAST TWENTY-FIFTH

The dedication of these chaplains and other wholesome influences prompted the *Phoenix Tribune* for May 17, 1919, to opine, "The soldiers of the 25th Infantry are men of high morals and we are pleased to have them in our midst." By mid-February 1926, the *Douglas Daily Dispatch* was likewise singing the praises of the garrison at Camp Harry J. Jones. In effusive terms, the reporter announced, "Douglas has within a mile of the center of the city a little unit of this great fighting machine. This unit is a battalion of the Twenty-Fifth Infantry." He concluded his laudatory remarks with the statement that "[t]he people of Douglas should have pride in this unit of the army that is here. This regiment was organized about 60 years ago and since that time the men who make up its forces have been engaged continually in working, studying and fighting to make their regiment one of the best and most dependable in the country. They have succeeded in a great measure."

STRAYING FROM THE FOLD

Regrettably, like other regiments throughout the U.S. Army, the Twenty-Fifth Infantry had its share of malcontents and scalawags. Murder topped the list of periodic crimes. As had been the case with other Buffalo Soldier units, men from the Twenty-Fifth sometimes turned on a comrade. For instance, two privates from Camp Little, Private Keyes of Company B and Private Kregel of Company C, "engaged in a shooting affray which resulted in the death of both" teenagers, who supposedly "had been quite friendly always," if the *Daily Morning Oasis* of May 25, 1919, was accurate. They would be among five victims within less than a month who died at the hands of a fellow member of the regiment.

In fact, homicides in Nogales did not end there. As the *Tombstone Epitaph* of June 15, 1919, noted a few days earlier, Private Carter of Company C, Twenty-Fifth Infantry, mortally wounded Corporal Hall of Company H. Carter claimed self-defense as he went to the post guardhouse.

Apparently, after that, killings ceased, at least until the spring of 1922. Then, as the *Prescott Weekly Journal-Miner* recounted on April 26, 1922, "Corporal Joseph M. Anderson of Company I, Twenty-fifth infantry, who was shot Saturday by Private William C. Dykes of the same company, died today [April 24] in Camp Stephen D. Little hospital. Dykes who, camp officers said, admitted the shooting and accused Anderson of intimacy with Mrs. Dykes, is alleged to have crept upon the corporal and fired four bullets into Anderson's body while the latter was sitting on his bunk." The account added that "Anderson, a long-distance runner and a basketball and football player, was one of the best athletes in the camp."

No clear-cut motive can be found for the January 1923 murder of Twenty-Fifth Infantry, Company K, private William Moore by William Williams. The assailant's attorneys successfully defended their client against a charge of murder. The jury returned a verdict of manslaughter. The court was asked for clemency.

Late in 1929, Thomas (also called Enos in another news account) Crockett, a cook in Company G of the Twenty-Fifth, fatally shot Sergeant Benjamin Mission of the same company. Crockett was jailed and charged with first-degree murder. The company commander stated that Mission, who was mess sergeant and the killer's superior, requested the removal of the cook from his kitchen duties. A resentful Crockett retaliated.

Usually exchanges between fellow enlisted caused the death of one or both of those involved in squabbles. An exception to the norm took place on November 9, 1918, when J. Velasco, an employee of the Sonora Bank and Trust Company, chanced on the body of Sergeant William J. White, Company K, Twenty-Fifth Infantry. The corpse lay behind the gas plant on Grand Avenue. The dead man still clutched a cigarette.

The afternoon before the murder became known, a white sentry heard a shot fired. Civilian witnesses also heard gunfire. One of them added that three men, two of whom appeared to be officers, had been seen. One of the officers seemed to be in pursuit of a Black soldier. A coroner's jury listened to the witnesses but could draw no conclusion as to who committed the crime.

That mystery was resolved. Lieutenant Brandon Finney of the Twenty-Fifth's machine gun company submitted his confession through a fellow officer. His confidant had witnessed the killing and presented Finney with an ultimatum. Either the killer must reveal his crime to the commanding officer at Nogales, Colonel Carnahan, or the witness would make known what he knew.

Finney revealed a sordid narrative: After he encountered White near the gas plant, the sergeant saluted but failed to remove the cigarette from his mouth. The lieutenant reprimanded the noncommissioned officer, who then proceeded to walk off. Incensed, Finney drew his sidearm and fired. Not waiting to learn of the consequences of his actions, he and a fellow officer who had accompanied him hurried back to Camp Little. Only afterward did they learn that White died from this cavalier deed.

With that, Finney was taken into custody, under house arrest since the morning he met with the colonel. Rather than stand trial in a Nogales court, he was to appear before a court-martial. The African American–owned *Phoenix Tribune* of December 28, 1918, reacted unfavorably to the handling of Finney's case: "the civil authorities refused to put him in the local Jail, declaring that they did not want it torn down. Later the lieutenant was taken to Douglas for incarceration." The fact that the matter would be handed by court-martial evoked the opinion that "happenings as these and others prove conclusively that white men should not serve as officers over colored soldiers."

Another white man, in this instance customs officer Jack Doolittle on duty in Nogales, also suffered light consequences. In 1928, he fatally shot one of a trio of Twenty-Fifth infantrymen who attempted to smuggle tequila from Mexico into the United States. Doolittle argued that one of the three men brandished a firearm, which provoked him to fire first. A coroner's jury subsequently determined that Doolittle's action was unjustifiable. His punishment, such as it was, entailed a transfer to Yuma.

Five years before, in December 1923, a woman who killed a soldier also escaped punitive measures. Louis Young of Nogales allegedly slayed Private Kenyon of Company H, Twenty-Fifth Infantry. The coroner's jury declared the shooting "justifiable homicide." It based its conclusion on evidence that Kenyon had forced his way into Young's home.

In other instances, the victim was not a soldier—instead, it sometimes was a family member. This was true for William Cushenbury (spelled "Cushenberry" in some accounts) with the Twenty-Fifth Infantry at Camp Little. He bludgeoned his spouse with a large knife and then he fled on foot. His capture by an officer and two enlisted men followed. On April 19, 1919, the *Border Vidette* of Nogales told the tale of William H. Cushenbury, "a soldier of the 25th Infantry [who went to]…the guard house at Camp Little. It is believed the soldier…is insane."

Although one bold headline exclaimed that the soldier committed a "SHOCKING UXORICIDE" when he stabbed his wife to death, a jury found him not guilty. During the hearing, the soldier accused a key witness for the prosecution, Louis C. Adams, of committing the crime himself. Cushenbury's attorneys also provided a masterful defense. One of his two lawyers spent nearly forty minutes arguing that the evidence left a reasonable doubt, which in a criminal case meant that a guilty verdict could not be reached. As the *Daily Morning Oasis* divulged on April 15, 1919, "At 6 o'clock P.M.…it was announced that the jury was ready to bring in a verdict." The turn of affairs meant that the defendant was returned from the jail. Once in court, the foreman handed "the verdict to the clerk, who recorded it and read it aloud to the jury." The judge questioned them whether they had reached their verdict. They replied in the affirmative. Then the judge dismissed the jury and set the defendant free. Cushenbury returned to the cell and gathered his personal effects. His attorneys drove him to the headquarters of his company at Camp Little.

Likewise, Jerry Robinson of the Twenty-Fifth engaged in an altercation with his spouse. The scuffle ended in what evidently was her accidental death. He struck her with such force that the unfortunate woman fell against a bedpost, thereby sustaining injuries that led to her death. One month later, in early July 1931, the court acquitted Robinson of manslaughter.

While Roberta Coates was not Private Charles W. Steven's spouse, they had a relationship. After discovering her with another man, Steven entered Coates's room and shot her. Then the Camp Little soldier turned the firearm around to shoot himself in the heart. Private Benjamin Curtis of Company B was another case of suicide, but this time, he shot himself in the presence of his wife and child. Curtis left a note for his comrades asking that they pay for his widow and orphan to be sent to San Antonio. Financial difficulties apparently triggered his drastic act.

The Twenty-Fifth Infantry's commanding officer's chauffeur at Camp Little resorted to a similarly desperate deed. Early in January 1926, charged with passing bad checks, young Private Clifton Brown killed himself, using a .38-caliber automatic pistol that sent a lethal round through his heart. A few days later, Private James Jones of the regiment's service company accompanied Brown's body to Baltimore, Maryland, for burial.

As tragic as these desperate deeds were, one of the most dire outbursts of violence occurred at Fort Huachuca. In late December 1932, the post served as the Twenty-Fifth Infantry's regimental headquarters.

At the end of the month, Private James H. Abernathy from the quartermaster detachment at the post wreaked havoc on three unsuspecting Twenty-Fifth Infantry officers and two family members. Inexplicably, Abernathy, who oversaw the post's gas station, discharged his .32-caliber pistol. The round killed Captain Joseph Wessely. Then the assailant seized the dead captain's car to drive to his victim's quarters. Once there, he shot Wessely's spouse.

His next victims, Captain and Mrs. David Palmer, also went down in a hail of bullets. A third Twenty-Fifth Infantry officer, Lieutenant Harvie R. Matthews, was the final target. Fortunately, he survived, but Abernathy did not. Arriving on the scene soon after Matthews's wounding, Corporal Peter Hardley, Company L, Twenty-Fifth Infantry, and a member of the provost guard, pursued and killed the murderer. Hardley's quick action ended the killing spree. It also silenced Abernathy, which meant authorities could not interrogate him in an effort to ascertain what prompted his murderous binge.

Motives for another killing, however, were evident. In 1938, Frank Connors from the Twenty-Fifth slew Nogales city clerk and treasurer Tracy Bird. Not surprisingly, at first, Connors pleaded not guilty, but he soon changed his statement to guilty and threw himself on the mercy of the court. The killer, a native of Prescott, Arizona, was only two years old when his father died. Two decades later, he faced life imprisonment or execution.

In November, he stood trial for the holdup and fatal shooting. The testimony of three witnesses and Connors's signed confession sealed the assailant's fate. He received the death penalty, which was to be carried out on February 10, 1939. A brief reprieve followed, sparing him for nearly seven months. After review by the Arizona Supreme Court, the three justices "affirmed the conviction of Frank Conner, colored, former Fort Huachuca soldier, condemned for the murder last October of Tracy Bird, former Nogales, Ariz., city clerk, and set his execution for September 22," as Nogales's *International* confirmed on July 15, 1939.

Thankfully, not all crimes rose to the level of loss of life. For instance, in late November 1932, Roland Blanton from the Twenty-Fifth Infantry spent ninety days in jail after he took an automobile in Nogales, Arizona, and drove it to Mexico. More than a year earlier, a Nogales jury acquitted another soldier from the Twenty-Fifth, Isadore J. Patterson, on the charge of perjury. In many respects, Patterson embodied the majority of his fellow infantrymen in the regiment, who abided by the law.

FAITHFUL TO THEIR TRUST

Indeed, like the other three Buffalo Soldier regiments, the men of the Twenty-Fifth tended to remain in uniform, faithfully serving for a number of enlistments and reenlistments. Among these stalwarts was First Sergeant George W. Jasper of Company F, Twenty-Fifth, who retired from the army after thirty years of service. Touted by Nogales's *International* on January 17, 1926, as "one of the greatest baseball pitchers ever connected with the regiment," he planned to leave army life and play for one of the teams "on the west coast of Mexico."

Other retirees elected to remain in Arizona. The Black American Legion Post No. 40 in Phoenix turned out to provide a proper funeral for veteran William Glass. The former first sergeant in the Twenty-Fifth Infantry was the first Black soldier to be "given a full military burial, according to the army regulations," or so claimed the *Phoenix Tribune* on August 25, 1923.

Perhaps not so accorded when he died in November 1933 was Arthur Brooks, who retired in 1928 from the Twenty-Fifth Infantry's service company. He remained in Nogales after leaving the army. Similarly, John Robert Carter took up residence in Arizona after his return to civilian life. Carter might be viewed as representative of the majority of those whose name, for decades, appeared on the Twenty-Fifth regimental roster. Born on November 18, 1890, in Petersburg, Indiana, he enlisted at Fort Sill, Oklahoma, at twenty-three years of age. For many years, he reliably performed his duties with Company C,

While few Tenth Cavalry soldiers died as a result of combat, deaths periodically occurred from a variety of causes. In such instances, their comrades gathered, as they did here at Fort Apache, to render customary honors such as the firing of a twenty-one-gun salute. *Courtesy the author.*

with which he came to Arizona in 1918. Originally, he reported to Yuma, but he soon transferred with his company to Camp Stephen Little in Nogales. Carter remained there from 1919 to 1920 and eventually reported to Camp Harry J. Jones in Douglas. He eventually went to Fort Huachuca. There he retired in 1943, after being credited with the thirty years in uniform that allowed him to receive his pension. Sergeant Carter died in January 1949, evidently at his last residence in Douglas.

MILITARY DUTIES

Between 1918 and 1940, what would have occupied the time of these veterans and their fellow soldiers while they still called the regiment home? For one thing, maneuvers regularly brought the Twenty-Fifth out from their posts, often in tandem with the Tenth Cavalry, to maintain their military edge. In the decades between the end of World War I and the United States' entry into World War II, infantrymen and cavalrymen periodically took to the field to engage in mock combat.

The routine varied. Sometimes, as in the summer heat of 1922, it entailed marching in full battle gear from Camp Stephen D. Little to Camp Harry Jones, some 150 miles on a taxing northeast route. For some unknown reason, however, the special orders from the War Department recalled the more than three-hundred-man forces after it had only made a few miles from Nogales.

Exercises in 1924 did take place as planned. Some 70 officers and 1,048 enlisted men from the Twenty-Fifth Infantry at Nogales and Douglas, along with the Tenth Cavalry from Fort Huachuca, headed to the pumping plant on the Santa Cruz River, seven miles northwest of Nogales. The Tenth rode westward, overnighting on the Parker Ranch in the San Rafael Valley. The next evening, they bivouacked at Patagonia. During the 1930s, when the Twenty-Fifth garrisoned Fort Huachuca and after the Tenth had transferred from Arizona, the regiment returned to its former home in Nogales. Two years later, they hiked through Sonoita and pitched their tents at the fairgrounds. From there, the unit continued on to Tucson.

During June 1940, the line of march passed Nogales's pumping plant and then went through Sonoita via the Circle Z Ranch and Patagonia. Another outing held in September of the same year took the Twenty-Fifth to Ruby and Walker Canyon west of Nogales.

After World War I, the Twenty-Fifth Infantry and Tenth Cavalry regularly took part in joint maneuvers at various locations in southern Arizona. *Courtesy the author.*

Sometimes, when a unit fell in and departed their post, such as Camp Jones, a small detachment remained to serve as a guard, along with some family members and a few stray dogs. That situation existed in early 1928 when the battalion posted to Douglas went east to a previous military border outpost, the Slaughter Ranch. As part of that outing, two to four biplanes flown from San Antonio were to be included, likely to be employed for aerial observation. At least that was the idea during May 1928, when one of the aircraft was to "work with the 'Reds' or invading army, while the other" accompanied "the 'blue,' or defending army" to observe "the 'enemy' as well as 'dive down upon them, simulating an attack with machine gun fire.'" In turn, the ground troops returned fire "using blank ammunition," reported the *Nogales International* on May 8, 1928. In February 1929, a similar scenario unfolded near Nogales when the Camp Little's Twenty-Fifth Infantry garrison staged a mock battle.

Seven years earlier, some of the infantrymen had a chance to observe the U.S. Army's C-2 dirigible. Additionally, a specially trained detail from the Twenty-Fifth received the assignment to moor the lighter-than-air ship as it halted in Nogales on its transcontinental flight from Langley Field Virginia to Arcadia, California. While C-2's westbound voyage succeeded without incident, on its return run eastward, while departing San Antonio, it burst into flames.

In the field, Twenty-Fifth Infantry enlisted personnel shared a "two-men" tent, as pitched here with a display of a soldier's combat gear from the 1920s. *Courtesy University of Arizona Library Special Collections.*

A few months later, a patrol from the Twenty-Fifth set out as one component of a search party for two missing U.S. Army aviators. Their plane went down in the borderlands after they departed San Diego. Cavalry contingents and other aircraft joined the quest for the downed airmen, who had been lost on December 7 on their way to Fort Huachuca. Despite extensive efforts, the land and air efforts never located the two officers or their remains.

A more positive outcome occurred in 1922 when the commanding officer of the Twenty-Fifth Infantry announced that 96 percent of the enlisted men qualified on the range after three months of practice. Supposedly, this was the highest percentile achieved by any regiment in the U.S. Army to that date. Happily, for the soldiers, those who made the mark would draw extra pay. In 1923, a major component from the Twenty-Fifth bested this record. As the *Phoenix Tribune* reported on June 30, 1923, "For the first time in the history of the United States an entire battalion qualified 100 per cent today on the rifle ranges." This was none other than the Twenty-Fifth Infantry's first battalion, qualifying at Camp Harry J. Jones.

Likely, Arizona national guardsmen benefited from this excellent marksmanship given that during 1922, soldiers from the state held joint annual maneuvers with the battalions of the Twenty-Fifth from Camp Harry Jones and Camp Stephen Little. In like manner, from time to time, both the Twenty-Fifth and Tenth Cavalry assisted in the training of

Left: While all soldiers received training at the firing range, a select few were designated as snipers. A Twenty-Firth Infantry private at Camp Little hefts a deadly scope-mounted Springfield rifle used for such purposes. *Courtesy University of Arizona Library Special Collections.*

Below: Hand-to-hand combat with bayonets also required regular drill for Twenty-Fifth Infantry soldiers. *Courtesy Fort Huachuca Museum.*

Citizen's Military Training Camp (CMTC) participants, who each summer from 1921 to 1940 took part in this program as a cadre to train reserve army officers in the event of war.

It was also in 1922 that both the Tenth Cavalry posted to Fort Huachuca and the battalion of the Twenty-Fifth Infantry at Nogales received word that they should be in readiness for protection of the railroad in the area. A strike that erupted in violence at Denison, Texas, concerned President Warren Harding's administration, but the need for mobilization did not arise.

PRIMARY MISSION CONTINUES

During its first years in Arizona, although a range of functions occupied the Twenty-Fifth Infantry, the border remained a significant part of their activities. As evidence, a detachment from the regiment left Nogales for three months guard duty in Ajo. Given that their base camp stood just over forty-miles north of Mexico, this position provided a secondary fallback to more immediate sites. In 1919, as indicated previously, the latter locations received considerable emphasis, evidenced by the ambitious construction project that ran from eastern Texas to western Arizona. The string of outposts represented a virtual wall where the garrison could respond rapidly to incidents at the nearby international line.

In that same year, calls for an actual barrier gained impetus. As the September 13, 1919 *Nogales Border Vidette* headline ran, some proponents called for "AN INTERNATIONAL FENCE" that would supposedly "End 'Reciprocal Rustling' of Cattle on Border." Members of the Arizona Livestock Sanitary Board championed "a horse high, bull-strong and practically man proof… international fence along the Mexican border." This group viewed "the cattle rustling situation on the Arizona-Mexico border" as a serious one that required "the attention not only of the state livestock board and their inspectors, but the military authorities as well."

The Twenty-Fifth's regimental commander retorted that although this was "not a military matter," he was willing to formulate a plan, working with cattle raisers from both Arizona and Sonora to end cattle running. A partnership on both sides of the border seemed necessary because, as one observer summarized, "A gang of Mexican rustlers come over and run off a lot of American cattle. Then a lot of Americans, who are only looking for an excuse, go over and run off a lot of Mexican cattle to get even." In the past, the physical barrier "seemed unlikely of accomplishment," but rustling reached such proportions that the idea was worth consideration. Admittedly, the fence would not offer a foolproof solution, but at least advocates argued that it would permit authorities "to track and capture both varieties of bandits, because they would have to cut the fence to make a raid, and would be easily tracked from the point where they crossed the line."

Besides the indiscriminate theft of herds in Mexico and the United States, the Twenty-Fifth Infantry continued to confront a number of border assignments. A petition circulated by the citizens of Ruby supported by other groups and individuals demonstrated continued concerns. The gist of their request appeared on September 3, 1921, in the *Border Vidette*: "Protection for American Citizens on Mexican Border at Ruby, Arizona." The body of the text emphasized "the killing of Postmaster and Mrs. Frank J. Pearson by Mexican bandits…and the killing at the same place of the Fraiser Brothers" the year before murderous raid. The petition went on to say:

> *Whereas there is a regiment of soldiers stationed at Nogales, and an unused army camp at Arivaca, 12 miles from Ruby, therefore the undersigned, for the purpose of obtaining protection for American life and property, request that a detachment of soldiers be stationed at Ruby, until such time as Mexican officials show a disposition to bring bandits to justice or attempt to capture or deport, or deliver, to American authorities, fugitives from justice who flee into Mexico after perpetrating crime in the United States.*

Elsewhere, in May 1921, the Twenty-Fifth Infantry went on alert after violence erupted in Nogales, Sonora. Mob rule and disorder triggered by the arrival of seventy-six Chinese and two Hindu laborers from Hong Kong provoked reactions by local Sonorans. If the unrest spilled over into Arizona, most particularly because of indiscriminate firing across the line, the U.S. infantrymen would be ready to respond.

The recommended forerunner of "The Wall" remained an unfulfilled concept until generations in the future. Nonetheless, its *raison d'être* extended beyond the stealing of steers and cows. While armament smuggling may have decreased, the illicit traffic in other goods across the border plagued civilian and military enforcement that long existed in the borderlands. This included liquor, a commodity that grew in importance after the passing of the Eighteenth Amendment by the U.S. Congress in 1919. Lawmakers called for the prohibition of making, transporting and selling alcoholic drinks. In that year, the requisite number of states ratified the amendment to launch the "noble experiment," as President Herbert Hoover dubbed the measure. In fact, Arizona was one of the first states to do so.

Good intentions aside, an array of criminal activities that included widespread bootlegging and smuggling from Canada and Mexico emerged. It was the southern source that kept the army active both in interdicting the flow of liquor and, as has been seen, sometimes in being a source of production or trafficking in the forbidden beverage. This source of criminal activity remained through December 5, 1933, when the Twenty-First Amendment repealed Prohibition. Even before the reversal of this double-edged effort at national temperance, the *Nogales International* noted on August 19, 1933: "The bar at Fort Huachuca is reported to be doing a flourishing business, selling beer to the soldiers of the 25th Infantry."

Possibly in an effort to curb inebriation, the Twenty-Fifth Infantry's colonel headquartered at Fort Huachuca endeavored to keep his men occupied. As a reporter in the May 14, 1936 *Brewery Gulch Gazette* wrote from Bisbee, "Some of the enlisted men feel sometimes that he goes a little bit too far with his ideas of how much work a man should do and occasional growls are heard. A couple of enlisted men were working on the parade ground picking up loose stones." One of them quipped, after they finished cleaning parade ground, that the next thing the colonel might concoct would "be setting out some brass trees and we'll have to keep them all polished up."

ERA OF GOOD WILL

Such levity could be indulged because, by the early 1920s, troops from the Twenty-Fifth Infantry lived a relatively quiet, routine existence. Rather than considering forces south of the border as potential enemies, in mid-January 1922, the regiment's battalion at Camp Little fell out for a review by officers from Mexico. As reciprocity, the battalion's commander, Lieutenant Colonel Robert H. Wescott, went to Nogales, Sonora, to observe the Mexican troops parading there.

By the fall of 1923, restoration of normalcy between the two neighboring countries was advanced further. When news that diplomatic relations between Washington, D.C., and Mexico City resumed, Nogales commemorated the good tidings with a major parade headed by the Twenty-Fifth Infantry band, which played on both sides of the border. Continuing along similar lines, the June 7, 1924 issue of El Centro,

Replete with white leggings, cap covers and cross belts, the Twenty-Fifth Infantry band made a distinct appearance. *Courtesy Fort Huachuca Museum.*

California's *Imperial Valley Press* announced, "The Republics of Mexico and the United States joined hands across the border today. Mexicans and Americans mingled in friendly intercourse, crossing and re-crossing the line at will, parading bedecked streets adjoining in a general welcome to President Álvaro Obregon, of the southern republic." Mexico's chief executive received a warm welcome. Once again, troops of the Twenty-Fifth Infantry traveled to Nogales, Sonora. There they joined counterparts from the Mexican army in a joint parade to honor President Obregon.

TO BE OR NOT TO BE

Even before reaching détente, in 1920, the removal of infantrymen as military border guards came in advance of future troop relocations and reductions. These martial movements had an impact on the region's economics and politics, much to the chagrin of communities affected by the change in the military status quo. Rumors reported as early as July 20, 1923, in the *Winslow Mail* opened with headline, "ARMY CAMPS MAY BE MOVED FROM THE BORDER." The possibility "of the abandonment of most if not all the army camps along the southern Arizona border" raised apprehensions. Withdrawal from

Arivaca, Ruby and Lochiel initiated the gradual consolidation. Next came Naco, which monetarily became a sub-post of Fort Huachuca before final occupation by a detail from the Twenty-Fourth Infantry before complete closure in 1924. Trepidations that the fort itself, along with Douglas and Nogales, might fall prey to the war department's growing perception that "no further need of troops along the border for police duty" existed save "a small detachment centrally located for use in emergencies" circulated through these communities.

Temporarily, military authorities forestalled further actions. Indeed, the Nogales's *International* on January 10, 1926, announced that the town would be would be assured a permanent post if it purchased a suitable site. The location consisted of the Saxon ranch and the old aviation field adjacent to the forest reserve. Once the real estate became available, the men of the Twenty-Fifth could undertake construction.

Regimental commander A.J. McNab reminded townsmen that the annual $1 million military payroll would be a strong incentive to act. He implied that time was of the essence when he added that "the only reason the 25th Infantry had not been moved to Cheyenne, Wyoming, sometime ago is because the government hasn't had the money to stand the expense of removal. He intimated that if something is not done soon by the city of Nogales, the present session of Congress may make an appropriation for the removal of the troops from Nogales to Cheyenne, Wyoming."

A few years later, the army's fiscal woes worsened when the Great Depression swept across the nation. As part of efforts to economize further, soldiers of the Twenty-Fifth along with all their comrades in the U.S. Army suffered a 15 percent cut in pay. Even with reduced funds, a presence remained desirable for more than just defense purposes. After the stock market's 1929 crash sent the nation into a financial tailspin, every source of income proved crucial to communities such as Nogales and Naco. Little wonder that continued speculation that troops would be sent elsewhere caused considerable concern.

By 1931, Nogales's two newspapers, the *Border Vidette* and *International*, were carrying numerous stories warning against drawdowns at Camp Little. One such report from the former periodical appeared on September 5, 1931, announcing the possible relocation of Companies F and G of the Twenty-Fifth Infantry to Omaha, Nebraska, thereby leaving only four companies at the camp. Supposedly, as the *International* speculated on September 12, 1931, the two companies would stay until October 1. It also seemed possible that white troops eventually would replace the men of the Twenty-Fifth, and

Above: By the early 1920s, Camp Naco's utility as a military outpost had ended. Before the installation's closure, Company A, Twenty-Fifth Infantry, was one of the last U.S. Army units to garrison the complex. *Courtesy Fort Huachuca Museum.*

Right: While posted to Camp Stephen Little in Nogales, the Twenty-Fifth Infantry appeared at numerous public events, including the community band stand, where the regimental musicians periodically performed. *Courtesy University of Arizona Library Special Collections.*

perhaps the same would be true for Fort Huachuca, where "white cavalry from Fort Clark, Texas" might substitute for the "Tenth Cavalry recently ordered scattered to points in the middle west."

Instead, by the end of the year, these pronouncements had given way to a grim reality when the War Department reached a definitive decision. The Twenty-Fifth Infantry's first battalion at Douglas's Camp Harry Jones and a second battalion of the same command at Nogales's Camp Stephen D. Little were to be consolidated at Fort Huachuca between May 1 and June 30, 1932. The third battalion already occupied the fort, which meant that at long last the entire regiment would be stationed at one post. In turn, Camps Jones and Little were to be abandoned.

Among others, Arizona's governor, G.W.P. Hunt, strongly protested the plan. He wrote to General Douglas MacArthur, chief of staff of the U.S. Army, as quoted in the *Border Vidette* of December 12, 1931, "Our defense will be weakened." The governor added, "I believe the move will be a serious strategic mistake." If need be, Hunt noted that he would call out the Arizona National Guard if "incursions from extraneous sources is a duty owed to our citizens by the federal government."

Not surprisingly, Governor Hunt's efforts to reverse the tide received widespread support. These protestations went beyond General MacArthur to the commander in chief, President Herbert Hoover. Word came that the loss of the battalion at Nogales would not take place during 1932. Similarly, Douglas would be spared. Evidently, lobbying by chamber of commerce members along with one of Arizona U.S. senators, Carl Hayden, and a host of others postponed action. That reprieve ended with the final pronouncement that by early January 1933, both battalions would pack and move to Fort Huachuca.

A hopeful projection that Camp Little's buildings would be retained in the eventuality that another regiment would be dispatched as replacements never materialized. The best that could be expected were temporary arrivals of the Twenty-Fifth in Nogales as part of annual maneuvers. For instance, a brief reappearance of the former garrison of Camp Little occurred in 1933 and 1939. In 1939, the *International* of April 29 warmly greeted the news of "1400 Soldiers Coming Here Next Week." Their encampment "on their old home grounds—Camp Little—where they lived for many years prior to abandonment of the local army post," would coincide with the fourth annual Nogales Fiesta. Happily, once again, "the famous 25th Infantry Band" would be there to participate in the annual fiesta parade." An advertisement in the May 6, 1939 *International* even welcomed the troops

After the Twenty-Fifth Infantry arrived at Fort Huachuca, the regimental mascot, "Myrtle," lived a long, comfortable life as a pampered pet. *Courtesy Fort Huachuca Museum.*

and all other visitors and enjoined them, "When you return home, tell your friends about Nogales—The City of Hospitality." It seems that this message was not lost on Chaplain and Mrs. Louis A. Carter; after the military minister retired, the couple intended "to locate in Nogales," according to the June 10, 1939 edition of the *International*.

Nogales also became home to several veterans from the Twenty-Fifth. Two decades earlier, Nogales's *Daily Morning Oasis* of November 2, 1919, reflected the generally more tolerant attitude that prevailed in Ambo Nogales. An *Oasis* reporter indicated that after a Black veteran had received his honorable discharge and sailed from France, he returned home. After his arrival, he visited "relatives in a town in the northern states. While passing through the central part of the city, he was attacked by a gang of toughs, hammered into unconsciousness, and left on the sidewalk, an inert heap."

Once the victim regained consciousness, "he expressed a natural surprise at the conduct of his assailants. He was wearing his uniform at the time also his wound stripes, and thought that they would be, at least, a guarantee of safety. He had fought to protect his fellow-countrymen for three years, and

Many men of Company C, Twenty-Fifth Infantry boasted long, honorable service records when they transferred from Hawaii to Arizona in the 1920s. *Courtesy University of Arizona Library Special Collections.*

had started a considerable time before they had thought of participating. So he had expected to be safe on reaching America."

The writer lamented, "Perhaps he would have been safe in Nogales. But this did not happen here. It happened in Chicago, and the wounded soldier was a colored man. The thugs who permitted the outrage disapproved of his complexion, and complexion has of late been a frequent pretext for murder in that enlightened town."

The article concluded with the admonition, "Nogales don't try to be a metropolis. Washington is one—Chicago is another. It is hard to pick out the ideal that we should copy; there are not many ideal cities. At all events we can find places to classify as awful warnings. We do, at least know what to avoid."

Thus, it appeared that more than fiscal matters bound together the civilians and military residents of Nogales. Apparently, a degree of mutual respect and acceptance could be found there that was not always present in the racial climate of the times. Nevertheless, money played a part in the equation. As the *International* of December 2, 1933, surmised, half the one hundred workers employed on construction projects at Fort Huachuca were from Nogales. While positive news, the temporary employment paled when compared to the revenue received when a battalion of the Twenty-Fifth occupied Camp Little.

Possibly, some of the workforce also was drawn from Douglas, whose community coffers decreased with the abandonment of Camp Jones. As Bisbee's *Brewery Gulch Gazette* of January 6, 1933, caustically commented, the loss "of several hundred troops, one battalion of the 25th infantry" from "our neighboring city, Douglas, is starting off the new year weeping and wailing." Facetiously, the *Gazette* commiserated: "While it is very painful to us in Bisbee to see Douglas suffer through the loss of troops, due to the fact that they have been moved to Fort Huachuca, we will try and bear up under this load of sorrow." In fact, the abandonment of Douglas's Camp Jones and the concomitant expansion of Fort Huachuca benefited Bisbee. The *Gazette*'s sharp attitude added further insult to the suffering Douglasites.

LULL BEFORE THE STORM

Once conjecture gave way to actual merging of all the scattered elements from the Twenty-Fifth Infantry, a status quo antebellum came into existence. Through the end of the 1930s, as the *International* on April 2, 1938, affirmed, Fort Huachuca was "the last of Arizona's string of frontier posts," while the Twenty-Fifth Infantry stationed there remained "the only active colored combat regiment in the Regular Army" of the six units established in 1866. What was more, as the African American–owned *Arizona Gleam* for February 12, 1937, proudly pointed out, the post and the regiment were "steeped with the traditions of the old West." The latter entity boasted "one of the most interesting histories of all units in the nation's regular army, being more than 67 years old...it became an integral part of the U.S. Army on April 20, 1869 in New Orleans. During its existence the 25th Infantry has seen service in nearly all American engagements and scores of its members wear service bars symbolic of numerous activities in which it has taken part."

Now, after nearly seven decades, "many of the men in the regiment" had served three or more enlistments, upholding a "tradition of army life" long extant in the Twenty-Fifth. The writer underscored, "The average length of

The Twenty-Fifth Infantry's coat of arms received approval on December 30, 1921. The insignia consists of an azure shield with a stone blockhouse representative of service at El Caney, Cuba. "Onward," the regimental motto, appears below. *Courtesy the author.*

service of the members is 7½ years, that of first class privates 13½ years, corporals 15 years and sergeants between 20 and 30 years."

As such, the article ended with the suggestion that Fort Huachuca presented "a pleasing and home-like appearance with its tree-lined streets, officers' family quarters and spacious quarters." The post now offered "an interesting place to visit, either for short or all-day inspection trips. Officers and men alike have been instructed to welcome visitors and make their stay as pleasant as possible."

Annual Army Day public celebrations indicated that the garrison honored this order. The one held during the spring of 1938 by the Twenty-Fifth Infantry offered visitors "demonstrations in gunnery and tactics," as well as included "displays of arms and equipment," all capped off with a barbecue luncheon and a regimental review. The following year's Army Day was hosted on April 6, following a similar schedule along with drills and a band concert.

At last, it appeared that Fort Huachuca and the Twenty-Fifth Infantry would enjoy a lengthy association. A few months after Army Day in 1939, water, long a matter of interest in the desert Southwest, presented an intimidating challenge. Draught and the springs that had supplied Fort Huachuca for four decades gave rise to the consideration of an alternative.

Once more, Nogales residents saw a glimmer of hope to recapture the regiment. The army could return to its former home of old Camp Stephen D. Little free of charge for the land. In particular, they looked toward Wirt G. Bowman, Democratic national committeeman, to use his party influence with Franklin Roosevelt's administration. The clarion cry of "Let's Get an Army Post!" raised spirits. Even if the regiment encamped for only "a few weeks stay," their presence "would stimulate business and there is always the probability that once they are here they might remain permanently," offered the *International* on June 24, 1939.

The paper further chided, "The worst blunder this community ever made was when it took more or less of an indifferent attitude toward the army post and the troops were moved away several years ago. Had every effort possible been made we are of the opinion the army post would never have been abandoned."

Fortunately for the fort, the military resolved the water shortage problem. This dashed the dream of a return to the days when men wearing the insignia of the Twenty-Fifth were a regular fixture in the area. Not only did the unit remain at Fort Huachuca, but it also was to be joined by thousands of other Black soldiers when the specter of another world war again threatened.

CHAPTER 5

WORLD WAR II

"THE DOUBLE-V"

WAR CLOUDS GATHER

As the September 9, 1939 edition of the African American–owned *Phoenix Index* indicated to its readers, "For months your press, your pulpit, your political leaders have been shouting for an equal opportunity in the armed forces of your country with but little result." As the reporter went on to observe, only four regiments of Black soldiers remained in the U.S. Army, along with two National Guard units, the Eighth Illinois and the Fifteenth New York. All six units were staffed to capacity. This meant that there was a "long waiting list of applicants," who although were "willing and anxious to serve" were refused enlistment "by a country badly in need of more regulars."

Indeed, of these half-dozen regiments, only one remained capable of immediate combat deployment. During a time when the Nazi *blitzkrieg* once again precipitated another world war, this sole surviving Black military, battle-ready organization was the Twenty-Fifth Infantry. Consolidated for posting at Fort Huachuca from Douglas and Nogales, much to the chagrin of those two civilian municipalities, the Twenty-Fifth, as in the past, continued to juggle military preparedness with community involvement. On one hand, whether present at the nearby Sonoita fairgrounds, where the regimental band turned out for the annual spring horse show, cattle show and horse races, participating in Bisbee's Fourth of July parade or outside southern Arizona contributing $170 in memberships to the NAACP, the men of the Twenty-Fifth remained a fixture in the region. Likewise, maneuvers, particularly during June and September 1940, also made the unit visible to locales in the San Rafael Valley to the pumping plant, seven miles north of Nogales, the Sonoita district via Circle Z Ranch and Patagonia, as well as at Ruby and the one-time Civilian Conservation Corps camp in Walker Canyon. In between parading and practicing the art of warfare, the troops played various sports and enjoyed off-duty pursuits, some of which were wholesome and others not.

A NEW DAY DAWNS

These days represented the proverbial quiet before the storm. As the United States edged toward entry into World War II, the operations tempo heightened. After the December 7, 1941 attack on Pearl Harbor, the pace accelerated with unprecedented velocity. As the *Nogales International* for December 12, 1941, announced, quick action around Arizona included the posting of extra military guards "at the Tucson army bomber base" (the origins of Davis-Monthan). Four days later, the noted three hundred troops

An infantry company from the Ninety-Second Division smartly marches out as it trains for the Second World War. *Courtesy Fort Huachuca Museum.*

from the Twenty-Fifth Infantry arrived for "patrol duty at the reservoirs, the pumping plant, and plant of the Citizens Utilities Company. A similar number was sent to Douglas." In due course, a few other military installations, such as one established at Papago Park in the Phoenix area, also added to the increase in the number of Black troops around the state.

The major wartime buildup for African American troops, however, centered on Fort Huachuca. As Stephen Smith concluded in *The African American Soldier at Fort Huachuca, Arizona, 1892–1946*, by 1941, everything at that post "began changing with dazzling speed." By the Second World War's end, the bucolic base near the Mexican border had been transformed into a bustling military post. Nearly 1,400 structures would house or support tens of thousands of segregated Black U.S. Army personnel, from the Thirty-Second and Thirty-Third Post Headquarters Companies, staffed by officer and enlisted members of the Women's Army Corps (WAC), to a pair of infantry divisions, the Ninety-Second and Ninety-Third. Both of these divisions traced their lineage back to World War I as part as the Allied Expeditionary Force dispatched to Europe. Reactivated on October 15, 1942, and May 15, 1942, respectively, the Ninety-Second and Ninety-Third gathered at what Tucson's *Arizona Daily Star* described on December 23, 1943, as an isolated, self-sufficient post "used exclusively for the training of Negro troops."

The new inductees joined old hands from the Twenty-Fifth. Maggi M. Morehouse underscored the nature of the new arrivals in *Fighting in the Jim Crow Army*. She summarized, "They came with college degrees and parole papers. They came with pockets full of loaded dice. They came damning America, her Jim Crow, and her lynch law. They came cursing Hitler and the Fascists and eager to do battle for human rights." Whatever their backgrounds, most found Fort Huachuca and southern Arizona a strange new home, especially because legions of them had just left their civilian world to don Uncle Sam's unfamiliar uniform and undergo the perplexing regimen of the military life. What probably was familiar to the majority of them was that they had been relegated to a segregated place just as they had experienced prior to entering the service.

In spite of this long-standing racist reality, Fort Huachuca became a mecca for Black units, as Smith recounted in *The African American Soldier*: "During Brigadier General Benjamin O. Davis's inspection in the summer of 1943, the following black units were at Fort Huachuca besides the two divisions: 336th Quartermaster Service Battalion; 560th Quartermaster Service Battalion; Detachment Quartermaster Corps; 310th Quartermaster

Black crewmen of tank destroyers learned the necessary skills before they shipped overseas for combat duty. Here they engage in a pleasant, unusual duty. Evidently, they were providing a tour for white USO volunteers, who have set aside their women's garb to don military coveralls for the occasion. *Courtesy Fort Huachuca Museum.*

Railhead Company; 406th Ordnance MM [Medium Maintenance] Company; 317th Ordnance MM Company; Ordnance Detachment SCU [Service Command Unit] 1922; HQ and HQ Detachment, 70th Ordnance Battalion; 734th Military Police Battalion; 750th Military Police Battalion; Detachment, CMP SCU 1922; Detachment, Medical Department; Medical Department (Veterinary Service); 714th Medical Sanitary Company; 268th Station Hospital; 29th Special Service Company; 17th Special Service Company; 37th Special Service Company; Post HQ Detachment (DEML) [Demolition] 1922d SCU; Engineer Detachments, SCU 1922; WAC [Women's Army Corps] Section, SCU 1922."

Also, reflective of one of the earliest missions performed by Black troops in Arizona, a detachment of military police kept "eternal vigilance, tact and intelligence in Douglas across from Agua Prieta." Some Black soldiers also served as guards at U.S. Army Air Force bases scattered around the state. On one occasion, Fort Huachuca's swing band and theatrical troupe entertained

Fort Huachuca's commanding officer and the band turned out to greet Brigadier General Benjamin O. Davis on his official visit to the home of the Ninety-Second Division. *Courtesy Fort Huachuca Museum.*

a group of Tuskegee Airmen sent for special B-25 training at the Douglas field, which became the city airport. As they familiarized themselves with twin-engine aircraft and instrument flying, they received ground support from the 335th Aviation Squadron consisting of Black personnel commanded by a white lieutenant.

To billet and provide for the needs of these staggering numbers, which on average totaled 25,000 individuals and at its height some 42,500 residents, Fort Huachuca evolved into "the third largest city in the state," while the Ninety-Third Division's "post newspaper," *Blue Helmet*, had the second-largest circulation in the entire state, issuing twenty thousand copies per week, as Smith noted. The other post newspaper, the *Apache Sentinel*, also reached a substantial number of soldiers along with many of the 1,400 civilians employed at the post.

An article in *Apache Sentinel* for October 1, 1943, was one of many that provided insight into the *zeitgeist* of the period. It seems that Private Perry Lightner of Charlotte, North Carolina, wanted to do his part to defeat the Axis. On March 17, 1943, at nearby Fort Bragg, he was inducted into the army. Lightner stated "his age as 19 because he did not know how old he was." Six months later, Lightner left the service with an honorable discharge from the army "because he was under age." The private was only sixteen years old.

Most of the legions of soldiers served out their entire enlistments. During their stay at Fort Huachuca, they engaged in many activities, such as the one announced in the March 27, 1941 Bisbee's *Brewery Gulch Gazette*. Army Day, slated for April 7, would include the recently formed 368th Infantry, which was the first of many other units established to reinforce the 25th. The paper mentioned that the public would have the opportunity to observe "the new equipment now being received, and the new formation recently adopted." This proposed program included "demonstrations of the uses of their various weapons and other equipment. Barracks, both of the older garrison, and in the new cantonment." Another addition included recently issued "motor vehicles for both regiments" that would bring an end to "both mules and horses" remaining in service on the former frontier fort.

OFF-DUTY PURSUITS

Besides the latest martial hardware, Black military personnel at the post continued to draw onlookers for athletic events. Baseball remained most popular. This included a game during Bisbee's 1941 Fourth of July celebrations. When playing at the fort, the fans could take their places at the eleven-thousand-seat baseball park. Moreover, they also would have a football stadium with sixteen thousand seats! Further, a pair of swimming pools, two gymnasiums, bowling alleys and numerous basketball courts where through the end of World War II 108 organized teams shot hoops dotted the military reservation. In addition, badminton, boxing, golf and softball all provided diversions.

Additionally, as Ulysses Lee singled out in *The Employment of Negro Troops*, the "the only full-time Theater [theatrical production]" in the army added to the quality of life at Fort Huachuca. Local productions as well as performances and appearances by many Hollywood personalities and some other celebrities, including heavyweight champion Joe Louis, enlivened the martial routine during off-duty hours.

For instance, as the June 18, 1943 Meridian, Mississippi *Echo* indicated, Joseph Louis Barrow, better known as the Joe Louis, the "Brown Bomber,"

had sewn on the chevrons of a sergeant during the war. The renowned heavyweight "paid a recent visit to the 92nd Infantry Division at Fort Huachuca, Arizona, and he gave the Division a fighting principal to take to the battle front." Speaking from the center of the post amphitheater, Sergeant Louis shared, "Discipline means everything to a fighter as well as to a soldier. Listen to everything you're told. Apply it to the best of your ability."

Of course, motion pictures were also screened at one of the five theaters. Perhaps even the 1943 feature *Marching On*—portions of which director and writer Spencer Williams, of the television series *Amos and Andy*, filmed at Fort Huachuca—might have been shown. Whatever the playbill, a racist symptom of the era marred the atmosphere. Preferential seating for white officers raised objections from the Black rank and file.

If these amusements were not sufficient, the post library offered books, newspapers and periodicals. Service clubs and the USO were provided. Additionally, squadron day rooms fitted up with a radio, magazines and newspapers and other distractions could be found. Also, many educational opportunities existed, from academic classes to a number of other lessons such as dancing, vocal training, art instruction and an impressive array of other activities that could occupy leisure hours. Music, including jazz and swing bands, proved popular and were performed and played at dances.

Opposite: From the 1880s through World War II, baseball reigned supreme as the preferred sport for Black soldiers stationed in Arizona. At one such gamed played at Fort Huachuca during August 1943, the Service Command Unit (SCU 1922) challenged the 92nd Division All Stars. *Courtesy Fort Huachuca Museum.*

Above: In addition to baseball, football grew in popularity particularly during World War II, as evidenced by this game at Fort Huachuca. *Courtesy United States Army Heritage and Education Center.*

Right: Ted "Double Duty" Radcliffe spent a brief time away from the Negro Leagues as a soldier in a Fort Huachuca ordnance unit. He soon returned to civilian life and continued his professional baseball career. *Courtesy the author.*

Enlisted personnel and officers danced in separate facilities. The latter group could take advantage of the segregated Mountain View Black officers' club.

All these efforts to maintain morals and, for that matter, morale were noteworthy. Nonetheless, the lure of greener pastures enticed some soldiers to leave Fort Huachuca for the adjacent burg of Fry. Prior to the extensive expansion of the post, the little community of 850 souls kept a drugstore and some mercantile operations where, in some instances, liquor could be purchased or enjoyed in a restaurant. All that changed when the garrison astronomically climbed. Once again, Stephen Smith's description proved apt. He painted a sordid picture of "a tent, trailer, lean-to and shack city of around 2,000, full of vice in the form of sleazy bars, violence, rampant prostitution, and gambling" as a successor to the infamous White City of yore. Violence, venereal disease and other unsavory situations frustrated the fort's commander and most fellow officers.

Post commander Colonel Edwin N. Hardy sought private funds to combat this pestilence. He wanted to create "a large amusement hall" that would "provide for dancing, drinking (nothing stronger than beer) skating, shooting galleries, restaurants, music" and wholesome women would provide dance partners and "put on floor shows," as Lee quoted in *The Employment of Negro Troops*. Even though the amusement casino, known as the Green Top, came into being, Hardy's scheme failed.

Good intentions aside, one of Hardy's greatest challenges remained: prostitution. Hardy failed to eliminate the main source of syphilis and gonorrhea, which adversely affected health as well as combat readiness. Publicly acknowledging this often-taboo subject, the March 24, 1944 issue

The segregated Mountain View Officers Club served only Black commissioned personnel and their guests. A separate club existed for white officers typical of the segregated society during the World War II era. *Courtesy Fort Huachuca Museum.*

of the *Apache Sentinel*, one of Fort Huachuca's many papers, noted, "Venereal disease is one of our most deadly enemies, not only in war-time, but also in time of peace. In wartime, it means a loss to the soldier in money, health and man hours of training." The article went into some detail about treatment and precautions, but the reality was that with so many thousand single men or men away from their families, the issue remained a critical one.

Colonel Hardy resorted to an unorthodox solution. Although contrary to War Department prohibitions, according to Stephen Smith's research, "the Hook" came into being, which was "a little cluster of buildings for military personnel" outside the fort's "north gate." The concept was, as Smith summed up in *The African American Soldier*, to establish

> *areas where prostitution was legal but under the eyes federal, state, and county health officials. There, infected prostitutes could be "put out of circulation" and treated, while men who entered the area would be required to use prophylaxis treatments. His plan was actually tried for a while. A fenced-in area along the fort's border was constructed and known prostitutes were moved into the enclosure. The prostitutes were examined by civilian doctors for any sexually transmitted diseases and once cleared, were given I.D. cards. Military police were stationed at the enclosure's gates and prophylactic stations were set up inside and outside the fence.*
>
> *…"The Hook," as it was called, produced the desired reduction in disease. But health officials complained that the area represented the Army's tacit approval of prostitution, and some in the African American community saw it as encouraging vice among the men, so the area was placed off-limits on August 22, 1943. The prostitutes quickly set up business out of their cars or trailers.*

Fort Huachuca also made efforts at prevention. For instance, as the October 22, 1943 issue of the *Apache Sentinel* pointed out, some of the output from the Special Service Silk Screen Shop included posters designed to educate soldiers concerning venereal disease. Of course, they tackled a wide array of other jobs "used in Army training programs—illustrating booby traps, reconnaissance and types of field maneuvers to posters on food."

Although the military attempted to curb the issue in and near Fort Huachuca, soldiers had other options to satisfy their desires. Admittedly, these alternatives all shared similar significant drawbacks. One of the closest places for diversion, Tombstone, was about twenty-five miles distant. Bisbee was thirty-five miles from the fort. Farther still, Douglas "was sixty miles away." Smith conceded, "Just across the border were the Mexican towns of Agua Prieta and Nogales offering a warm welcome to African American soldiers with much less prejudicial treatment." Another reference provided by Maggi Morehouse's *Fighting in the Jim Crow Army* quoted Black GI Howard Hickerson's recollection that Mexico afforded a place where a soldier could go to "kick up his heels," presumably without repercussions. Reinforcing this perception, another Black soldier posted to Arizona during the war, Bill Perry, recalled, "I could go to Mexico, but I couldn't go to town in the United States. I went to Tucson twice and then they cut it off." In contrast, a quieter venture across the border took place at Naco, Sonora, where according to the *Apache Sentinel* of April 28, 1944, several army wives enjoyed an outing to "the bordering Mexican town" organized by the USO. As part of the outing, "En route the group stopped to enjoy a picnic lunch at one of the highway picnic spots."

Often, trips north of the border and away from Fort Huachuca proved another matter. In *Fighting for Hope*, Robert Jefferson encapsulated the situation in larger cities, where soldiers "learned quickly to travel in groups, as they frequently found themselves embroiled in skirmishes against local police and white soldiers." Such an outbreak took place on June 14, 1942, at Tucson's American Legion Hall, where eight Black soldiers from Fort Huachuca came up against a city policeman and a detachment of white U.S. Army Air Force personnel from Davis-Monthan Field southeast of downtown. A few months before that, another duel flared up in Nogales between white military police and veterans of the Eighth Air Force. A combination of Black and white military police quelled the fighting without serious incident. Even so, Nogales became off limits after that.

More seriously, during late summer of 1942, Private Jessie Smith, a twenty-five-year-old, newly arrived recruit from Philadelphia, died in Flagstaff. Local law enforcement gunned him down in response to his supposed misconduct.

As the *Brewery Gulch Gazette* of January 15, 1942, wryly related, one approach to prevent such altercations included the rejection of a proposal by city leaders in response to the USO's plan "to build a negro recreation center in Tucson." Perhaps Tucson's city fathers believed that one way to prevent clashes was to make certain Black soldiers would not spend their leaves in town. Equally probable was sending a message that African Americans were not welcome in the community. Eventually, racist attitudes somewhat lessened, at least in Tucson. For instance, the *Apache Sentinel* on June 16, 1944, headlined an excursion for that forthcoming Sunday to the Old Pueblo for "a picnic and horseback riding the same afternoon." The 12th Street USO in Tucson, in tandem with the Fry USO, facilitated the festive plan. Another example of USO involvement to bring Fort Huachuca residents together with Tucson citizens, at least for the Black community, took place on Labor Day 1943. In this instance, townspeople traveled to the post.

The *Apache Sentinel*'s September 3, 1943 edition went into considerable detail:

> *A Labor Day picnic for which 50 of Tucson's most attractive and personable young women will be brought to Fort Huachuca and a scheduled Sunday afternoon broadcast over KVOA featuring Fort Huachuca talent are two of the things that were discussed by Post Special Service Division officials and USO representatives from Tucson in a meeting here last weekend. Representing the Twelfth Avenue USO Club in Tucson were Mr. Thomas Dent, director; Miss Eleanor Coleman, assistant director, and Miss Geraldine Powdrill, clerical assistant and a student at the University of Arizona. Also present during the discussions was Miss Margaret Knight, member of the Tucson USO board of directors and a prominent YWCA official.*
>
> *The USO committee and Special Service officials discussed a number of matters relative to better public relations between Fort Huachuca and Tucson as well as between troops stationed at this Post and troops stationed in the environs of Tucson.*
>
> *Mr. Dent is responsible for the inauguration of a half-hour all-Negro radio program on station KVOA, Tucson. The program is heard on Sunday afternoons from 2:30 to 3 o'clock. Recently it has featured brief speeches by prominent Negro Tucsonians and interviews of soldiers, Army wives and civilians.*

NO PEACEFUL HAVEN

While Tucson partially accepted the presence of Black soldiers, as GI Nelson Perry reinforced, other communities did not follow suit. As noted, this sometimes led to the military placing restrictions on a place such as Bisbee, where after a Black enlisted man was told in a local bar that "we don't serve niggers," the fight that erupted in response closed the town to soldiers. A more convivial attitude existed in Phoenix. From the start, the state capital generally offered an accepting atmosphere for Black soldiers, at least in certain portions of the segregated municipality. Outside of Fort Huachuca, the greatest concentration of African Americans in the state resided in or near there. By 1942, churches, businesses and various newspapers served the more than 4,200 African Americans. That number blossomed after another regiment consisting of 3,000 or so Black soldiers arrived in the metropolitan area.

Upon arrival in Arizona, the third battalion scattered to Douglas, Tucson, Nogales and Yuma for varied duties. In turn, the first and third battalion of the 364th Infantry (composed mainly of raw recruits from Chicago, Philadelphia and New York) reported to Camp Papago Park five miles east of Phoenix's downtown. Arriving in June from muggy Louisiana to the arid heat of Arizona, they served as guards for the German prisoners of war held at the camp. As Truman Gibson Jr. contended in *Knocking Down Barriers: My Fight for Black America*, the infantrymen were moved into "tarpaper shacks" that during the summer morphed from crude shelters to "sweltering furnaces."

The unit's leap from the Jim Crow South to the remote Southwest desert did little to assuage disgruntled soldiers. In describing Fort Dix, New Jersey, in the March 28, 1942 issue of the New York City *Amsterdam Star-News*, the depiction could have applied to the experience of the 364th. The editorial noted that Black soldiers held "a deep resentment against the vicious race persecution which they and their forbears have long endured. They feel that they are soon to go overseas to fight for freedom over there." In short, many of these Black soldiers subscribed to a concept articulated in 1942 by the African American *Pittsburgh Courier*: the "Double Victory" or "Double-V" campaign. Many in the African American community fought for a dual purpose under the slogan "Victory Abroad and Victory at Home"—the former goal to defeat the Axis overseas and the latter calling for equality in the United States.

Boredom and isolation added to the volatile mix. So, too, did the purported violent and highly racist nature of the regiment's executive officer, Lieutenant Colonel Hugh Adair. These factors might have fueled an act of defiance at Camp Papago Park when an estimated five hundred members of the regiment "refused to disperse when ordered to do so by the regimental commander," or so recounted Ulysses Lee. Perhaps seeking a means to quiet unrest in the ranks, the regimental commander made an about face. For Thanksgiving, he allowed the men to consume an unlimited beer ration. Truman Gibson added that the colonel "handed out plenty of passes." Many men took advantage of this break from military life. Unfortunately, this brief respite from Camp Papago Park coincided with higher command's new policy of replacing the 364th detail from its own ranks who served as military police (MPs), shifting the responsibility to the African American–staffed 733rd MP Battalion. A major repercussion resulted from this policy shift. The 733rd replaced men from the 364th who previously had been detailed to maintain law and order within the regiment. Despite the regimental commander's request to reverse the order, his protest went unheeded. And now, with the second battalion returning to the regimental ranks after their Thanksgiving meal, during which some of them became intoxicated, many of the men headed for the segregated Black neighborhood on Phoenix's eastside.

There, as described in *The Employment of Negro Troops*, "on Thanksgiving night of 1942, approximately 100 men of the regiment engaged in a shooting affray with a detachment of Negro military police…with the result that one officer, one enlisted man, and one civilian were killed and twelve enlisted men were seriously wounded." The soldiers were white First Lieutenant August J. Essman and Black Private George F. Hunter. The civilian, Robert Riley, also an African American, was the third of the confirmed fatalities.

A pair of articles in the *Arizona Republic* for November 27 and 28, 1942, provided the first news of the "minor war that raged over twenty-eight blocks of East Phoenix." The chaos exploded after irate infantrymen returned to camp, where some of them "broke into the armory and stole rifles, and machine guns. For a few minutes gunfire filled the air." Black MPs reinforced by white counterparts and local law enforcement stepped in to quell the outbreak. A scout car mounted with a .50-caliber machine gun joined the efforts to end the danger and apprehend the guilty parties.

Later, contradictory descriptions arose about the details of the exchange, but what is certain is the military response in the aftermath. The army launched an investigation into what became known as the "Phoenix Thanksgiving Riot." Brigadier General Benjamin O. Davis Sr. arrived as one of the investigators. According to the November 28, 1942 edition of the Washington, D.C. *Evening Star*, "A military board's investigation had resulted today in the arrest of more than 180 colored soldiers—the aftermath of a three-hour gun battle involving approximately 300 soldiers and 100 military and civil police."

Later, twenty-seven of these suspects stood court-martial, a process that lasted through early 1943. By March 25, as El Centro, California's *Imperial Valley Press* recapped of the defendants, "One man was sentenced to be hanged….Other sentences included one 50 year term, one 40 year term, one 25 year term, three 20 year terms and five 10 year terms. Three soldiers were acquitted, charges against another withdrawn, and three declared insane." The army withheld the condemned soldier's name until a final decision was made regarding whether the death sentence would be confirmed. As part of this process, a board of review considered the matter, as Detroit's *Michigan Chronicle* reported on April 3, 1943. The article ended with the opinion of Phoenix's chief of police, Don C. Steward, who "believed the riot stemmed from long-standing ill feeling between colored soldiers and colored military police. The disturbance was set off when a soldier was wounded resisting arrest after he had hit a colored girl on the head with a bottle."

What the *Michigan Courier* reporter failed to do was follow up with the fate of Joseph Sipp, the man slated for death. Evidentially, President Franklin D. Roosevelt commuted Sipp's sentence. Further, as Ray Stern recapped many decades later in the November 25, 2020 edition of the *Phoenix New Times*, "The amount of prison time the men actually served is unknown." He went on to reference the speculation of Paul Hietter, a Mesa Community College history professor, who was skeptical that the convicted soldiers served considerable time for their participation in the riot.

Regardless, after this outburst, the regiment temporarily remained in Phoenix. Surprisingly, the regimental band appeared in the March 1943 Rodeo Parade, indicative that the volatile situation had calmed. As an aside, many months before the so-called riot, which bespoke of the regiment making a positive impact on the community, the *Coolidge Examiner* of July 31, 1942, referred to the 364th Infantry Band as the "nationally famed musical aggregation." As a further indication of the respect the bandsmen seemed to have attained, they were slated to perform in the community's ambitious American Legion convention.

Such rare acknowledgment contrasted with a prejudice held by some Phoenicians. Consequently, this bigoted group must have been pleased to learn that the regiment received orders to relocate. During May 1943, the men were on the move. They rode the rails to Camp Van Dorn, Mississippi. At that post, friction continued. The events that followed the 364th's departure from Arizona would lead to misconceptions, mysteries, myths and outright fabrication, but exploration of that narrative remains for a future telling.

THE MARK OF CAIN

Besides these incidents of racial unrest and the three deaths in Phoenix, murder occasionally revealed the darker side of soldier life. Not surprisingly, these homicides occurred at Fort Huachuca or the adjacent community of Fry. That was so in early 1942 when three soldiers killed Carroll Quail, a Fry taxicab driver, and then took his vehicle as far as Texas. There, the three murderers and deserters—J.C. Levice, Charles Sanders and Brady I. Cole—abandoned the cab. Authorities soon apprehended them. Extradited to Arizona, they stood trial for first-degree murder. After they pleaded guilty, the trio received the death sentence, to be carried out on January 8, 1943, at Florence Prison's gas chamber.

Some eight months later, as the *Nogales International* for August 14, 1942, reported, "The brutally beaten body of Daniel E. Bass, 64, an employee of a service club bowling alley at Fort Huachuca" was discovered by fellow workers. Approximately $465 in cash also "was reported missing from the club, as military and federal authorities launched an investigation into the murder." A number of suspects underwent interrogation, but to no avail. The crime went unsolved.

Near year's end, no doubt existed as to who fatally stabbed Private Joseph Shields. His assailant, a private from the same division, James Rowe, stood court-martial for the slaying, which resulted over a pack of cigarettes. Nogales's *International*, this time on November 13, 1942, noted that Rowe "was found guilty and sentenced to be hanged." A trapdoor was installed in one of the warehouses on post, and after "all higher legally constituted reviewing authorities" contemplated Rowe's fate and confirmed the sentence, he went to the makeshift gallows. Rowe's body then was interred at the post cemetery.

A similar end came to Staff Sergeant Jerry Sykes. The old story of a love triangle resulted in the murder on the post of Hazel Craig, the spouse of a fellow NCO at the fort. The required review sustained the findings. On January 19, 1943, once more the warehouse trapdoor was sprung, and the body was buried at the post cemetery.

Yet a third candidate for the hangman, Oscar Dudely, awaited his date with death. Convicted of murdering a fellow soldier from the Twenty-Fifth Infantry in Montana rather than Arizona, Dudely nevertheless returned to Fort Huachuca for his court-martial. In later January 1943, he escaped the noose. He successfully fled to nearby Mexico. More than a decade passed when, in September 1954, Memphis police arrested him. After being fingerprinted, the police discovered that they had apprehended the condemned man. With Dudely back in the hands of the U.S. Army, a review board commuted his sentence to life imprisonment and confined him to the disciplinary barracks at Fort Leavenworth, Kansas.

LESSER PUNITIVE ACTIONS

Fortuitously, most crimes proved less serious than murder. In fact, if a letter to the editor printed in the *Apache Sentinel* on November 19, 1943, can be believed, the majority of the thousands of Black soldiers stationed at Fort Huachuca made that "military reservation…the most law-abiding community of its size and population in the State of Arizona. All one has to do to keep abreast of the times is to read the Arizona press and become convinced that there are fewer major crimes and certainly less misdemeanors at Ft. Huachuca among its military and civilian inhabitants than in the cities of Tucson, Bisbee, and even Phoenix, the capital of Arizona."

Truly, those who broke the rules for lesser infractions constituted the majority of the troops taken into custody, at least at Fort Huachuca. When arrested, the perpetrator could choose to be sent to the post stockade near the main gate or be taken to the Post Rehabilitation Camp, which, as Cornelius Cole Jr. described in *Fort Huachuca: The History of a Frontier Post*, "was removed from other post facilities. It was entirely under canvas—hospital tents for the messes, walled tents for administration, pyramidal tents for personnel, and canvas flies for kitchens." Those who volunteered for the "Rehab" camp were referred to as "students" rather than prisoners. No barbed wire or armed guards kept them in bounds. They remained in camp on the honor system and could even enjoy privileges such as attendance at motion pictures, sports events and the like if they earned these benefits through their conduct. While the results were mixed, for the most part, Smith concluded, "It worked."

POURING OIL ON WATER

Contrary to this considerable unrest, Fort Huachuca's commanding officer, Colonel Edwin Hardy, boasted in March 1943, "We have not had a single concerted action against authority, riots, or any racial clashes. The people of Arizona have come to be less prejudiced against Negroes and are showing more confidence in them." This positive picture deviated from later analysis of the atmosphere at the post. For instance, although with only vague citation of sources, Maggi Morehouse, in *Fighting in the Jim Crow Army: Black Men and Women Remember World War II*, portrayed a different version of Fort Huachuca during the Second World War. She contended that "relations between white officers and black enlisted men deteriorated" there. The text continued: "One white officer was hit in the head with a shovel when he was asleep in his tent, and a car of white officers was stoned as they drove off the base." Elsewhere, officers and men of the Ninety-Third clashed in the streets and bars of Nogales, Mexico. The Associated Negro Press reported, "Information trickled out of camp that several white officers including one colonel had been severely beaten up or killed in altercations with enlisted personnel. The officers are said to stand far behind the lines during firing practice with live ammunition because they fear a sharpshooter might train his sights on them and revenge mistreatment."

Mary Penick Motley's extensive, revealing interviews for *The Invisible Soldier: The Experience of the Black Soldier, World War II* added credence to the negative attitude held by many African Americans in the U.S. military of the era. Perhaps the most telling comment came from a physician serving with the Ninety-Second Division at Fort Huachuca. In no uncertain terms, Dr. Rudolph Porter candidly vouched, "In less time than it takes to change into a uniform a black man knew who the real enemy was, the United States military." Elsewhere, Motley quoted another veteran as recalling:

> *Things got so tense at Huachuca one time that they brought in General B.O. Davis, Sr., to pour oil on the troubled waters. I did not attend the closed session of the general and the men, but it was the talk of the fort. They felt that he had not come down to hear about their problems but to give a biographical run-down on how he had made it and to tell us to turn the other cheek. After his visit, the name of B.O. Davis, Sr., was synonymous with "yes-sirism" and "Uncle Tomism."*

Happily, while some soldiers questioned Davis's loyalties, Motley reported that there were other Black officers to be admired. One was a veteran of the Twenty-Fifth Infantry who, although he "had, comparatively speaking, little education…he had fifteen years' experience in automatic weapons and was an expert in their handling and a skillful teacher in their use.

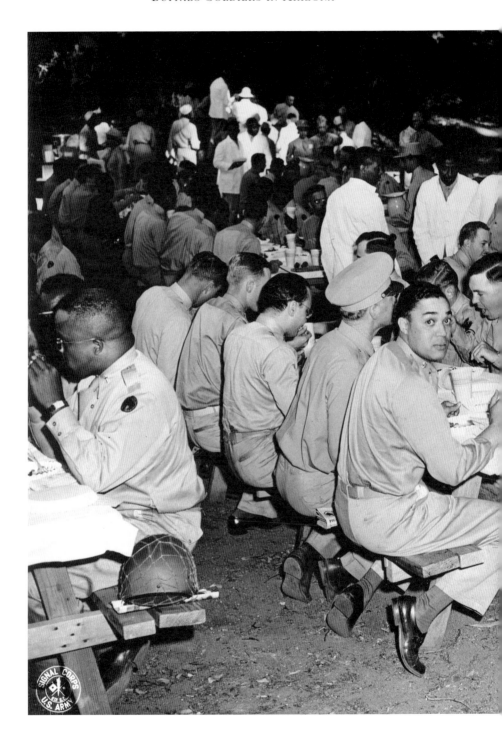

During late May 1942, Colonel Edwin Hardy hosted a picnic for all officers, both Black and white, "to create a moment of interracial understanding, at a distance from the training sites." Some six hundred officers and a select few civilians gathered at Huachuca Canyon for this informal effort, representing a rare occasion of integration. *Courtesy Fort Huachuca Museum.*

While he sometimes murdered the king's English explaining the weapons he always got his program across. The men understood him, and in action they followed him without question. No higher compliment can be paid an officer."

In contrast, despite his report that all was well at his garrison, Colonel Hardy perceived, as Pauline Peretz noted in *Une Armée Noire*, that many Black soldiers at Fort Huachuca held "a strong mistrust of him." Peretz went on to share:

> *One evening in May, Colonel Hardy and white officers from the 92nd left by car for Fry. They were stopped by a roadblock and men armed with bottles. One of the officers was injured in the eye and was hospitalized in the fort hospital. By leaving the military reserve, white commanders became more vulnerable, even if the law continued to be on their side. A white officer was also struck in the head by a soldier in his sleep; he would be treated at the Black hospital, a novel manifestation of his superiority. After these incidents, a rumor circulated around the fort: the white officers would be massacred as soon as the 92nd was sent into combat. But only these three incidents called into question the physical integrity and authority of white people. These were not necessarily warning signs of mutiny; moreover, no soldier was yet in possession of weapons or ammunition.*

Desirous of avoiding a major outburst of racial tension that recently plagued Detroit, Harlem and other cities, Hardy sought "dialogue," concluded Peretz. He believed that "the sharing of a conviviality between white officers and Black officers, more affected by the recent hardening of the racial treatment and the expression of racist prejudices." One example of an attempt to bring together Black and white commissioned officers arose from the staging of a Black art exhibit at segregated Mountain View Club, where Black and white officers and civilians joined to celebrate the opening of this impressive display. Jerome, Arizona–born muralist and emerging artist Lew Davis (no relation to the general) occupied a major role in this impressive tour de force. As an aside, later, he returned to Fort Huachuca as an enlisted man, eschewing a commission to remain true to his roots as the son of a carpenter in one of the mines in his hometown. At the post, he oversaw the impressive output of the silkscreen operation.

Davis's reporting for active duty postdated another of Colonel Hardy's efforts to maintain a degree of unit cohesion. In late June 1942, he organized a barbecue for all officers, both Black and white, where

Members of the Ninety-Second Division wore a shoulder sleeve insignia featuring a black bison encircled by a black border. The Ninety-Third Division, which served with the French army during the First World War, received an insignia that bore a blue French helmet. *Courtesy the author.*

military protocol temporarily would be suspended "to create a moment of interracial understanding, at a distance from the training sites," as Peretz indicated. Six hundred officers and a select few civilians gathered at Huachuca Canyon. Taking their places at wooden tables, the picnickers enjoyed an informal meal served by WAC volunteers. Hardy circulated among his subordinates and, after informally mingling with them, turned to a more formal address. He acknowledged the recent arrival of the new division and its officer, which made "it is necessary that we know, appreciate and respect ourselves in a spirit of generosity and benevolence in order to be able to work effectively together." This was no easy task, but inroads into better relations grew out of the World War II experience. Yet years remained before the U.S. military finally integrated, and more years elapsed before the nation followed suit.

FROM SOLDIERS TO ARIZONA CIVILIANS

Although no longer located in Arizona as military organizations, some Buffalo Soldiers remained after the troops departed. George Thompson was among those soldiers turned civilians. On August 8, 1941, the *Coolidge*

Examiner ran a headline: "Aged Negro with Unusual War Record Lives Quietly on Desert." The story that followed told of the old Twenty-Fifth Infantry enlisted man who surreptitiously enlisted as an underage sixteen-year-old. His decision to join the army led to a life of "adventure, danger and excitement." Between "his period of service, which was continuous from 1884 to 1905," Thompson claimed to have been wounded "13 times and earned the nickname 'Brass' because of its unmistakable qualities portrayed in himself."

Likewise, native Alabaman Chaplain Louis Augustus Carter and his spouse found Arizona sufficiently agreeable that after his military ministry concluded with a much-deserved 1939 retirement and tribute dinner, the Carters set off to Nogales, Arizona. Unfortunately, the couple enjoyed little time together in their adopted home. Not long after Reverend Carter's admission to the Veterans' Administration Hospital in Tucson, he died. As the July 5, 1941 edition of the *Phoenix Index* indicated, he received the last rites warranted by his commitment to his soldiers. Flags flew at half-staff at Fort Huachuca. His mortal remains were laid to rest with full military honors at the post cemetery, where he lies along with some of his soldier flock. During the Second World War, the chaplain's son, Lieutenant Booker Carter, received a commission. His widow, Mary Moss Carter, shared the chaplain's concern for the troops in his congregation. After the death of her spouse, she volunteered as a hostess at Guest House No. 1 in the fort's "New Cantonment."

After honorably serving with the Twenty-Fifth Infantry from 1915 to 1923, Lucius Franklin Monroe Jackson made his home in Nogales, Arizona. Another Alabama native, Jackson would travel thousands of miles from his home town of Eufaula far across the Pacific. In 1915, while stationed at Schofield Barracks in Hawaii, he was assigned temporary duty along with many other men from the regiment who built the Mauna Loa Trail. Afterward, he transferred with the Twenty-Fifth to Camp Little in Nogales, Arizona. While there, as his descendants attested, Sergeant Jackson "fell in love" with Nogales and married Angela Perez, a native of Sinaloa, Mexico. They made their family home on East Street, the last house on the hill that sat on the border, only yards from Mexico.

Here they raised eight children and welcomed twenty-one grandchildren, many of whom assumed positions as prominent community leaders. For instance, Jackson's youngest son, John, became the first Black/Afro-Mexican citizen elected to the Nogales City Council; he also served as vice-mayor. Many of the Buffalo Soldiers who made Nogales their home married local women, mostly Mexican nationals, and raised biracial families. In 1928, Jackson and fellow Buffalo Soldiers established the first school for Black residents in Nogales, the Grand Avenue/Frank Reed school for grades K–8.

MEMBERSHIPS, MEMORIALS AND MUSEUMS

Happily, some of these descendants of Buffalo Soldiers still live here or occasionally return to celebrate their ancestors. Beyond them, other flesh and blood reminders of Buffalo Soldiers remain in Arizona. Reenactors likewise offer living links to the past, as do, over the years, upward of a dozen groups with members who identify in diverse ways with the Buffalo Soldiers. Motorcycle clubs ride in leathers adorned with symbols and bold lettering proclaiming an affinity to African Americans in the U.S. Army stationed in the state. Other organizations, sometimes affiliated with national associations and, in other instances, strictly regional or local in nature, exist to promote an array of goals. They engage in such activities as granting scholarships to worthy students, providing educational programs, gathering descendants together and erecting monuments or statues to commemorate the deeds of the Black troops they admire.

On May 3, 2021, more than a decade of determined efforts culminated in the dedication of Tucson's Buffalo Soldier Memorial Plaza. Located at the Quincie Douglas Neighborhood Center, the adjacent public library houses several titles related to the Black military experience. *Courtesy Greater Southern Arizona Area Chapter Ninth and Tenth Horse Cavalry Association.*

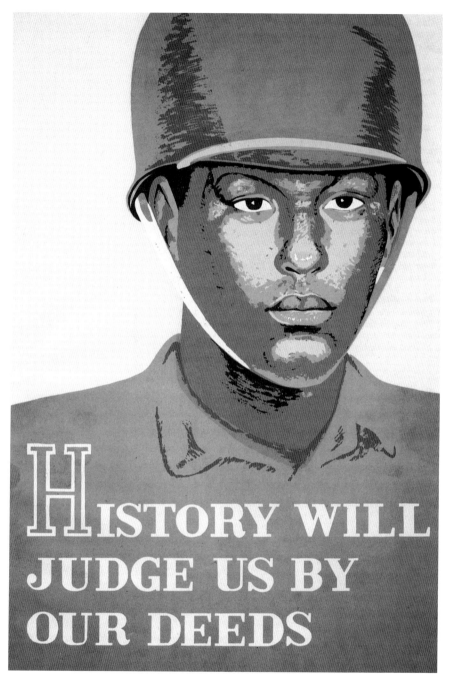

During late May 1942, a poster designed by Arizona-born artist Lew Davis read, "History Will Judge Us by Our Deeds," a statement and image to promote esprit among Black troops serving in World War II. *Courtesy Fort Huachuca Museum.*

In 1977, Fort Huachuca's centennial celebration spotlighted the dedication of a heroic bronze Buffalo Soldier statue. This was one of the first such memorials commemorating the Black soldiers' history in the West. *Courtesy Fort Huachuca Museum.*

Besides these bronzes and outdoor memorials, additional interpretive means help keep the Buffalo Soldier memory alive. Additionally, exhibits presented around the state trace various aspects of a complex, compelling story. Also, Camp Naco, once designated by the National Trust for Historic Preservation as "one of America's 11 Most Endangered Historic Places," now is being resurrected by an impressive public-private partnership. Further, a larger-than-life figure serves as the centerpiece for of Fort Huachuca's Buffalo Soldiers Park. Another memorial adjacent to Tucson's Quincie Douglas Neighborhood Center chronicles the deeds of these African American patriots. Consequently, an impressive legacy remains in the forty-eighth state, which might well deserve the title "The Traditional Home of the Buffalo Soldier."

BIBLIOGRAPHY

Archival Material

Carter, John Robert. Papers, 1913–24. MS 326. University of Arizona Libraries, Special Collections. Tucson, Arizona.

Programme Farewell Service and Exercise for Louis Augustus Carter Colonel, Chaplain Corps, U.S.A. Fort Huachuca, Arizona, October 29–30, 1939. Fort Huachuca Museum, Sierra Vista, Arizona.

Records of the U.S. Adjutant General's Office: Returns from U.S. Military Posts, 1800–1916, Nogales, Arizona, RG 94. M617 Roll 866. National Archives and Records Administration.

Records of U.S. Army Continental Commands, 1821–1920, RG 393. National Archives and Records Administration.

Returns from Regular Army Cavalry Regiments, 1833–1916, RG 393. National Archives and Records Administration.

Returns from U.S Military Posts, 1800–1916, RG 393. National Archives and Records Administration.

White, Joseph. "Diary 1888–1893." AZ380, Special Collections, University of Arizona Library. Tucson, Arizona.

Government Documents

Annual Reports of the Secretary of War, 1866–1906. Washington, D.C.: U.S. Government Printing Office, 1866–1906.

A Historical Analysis of the 364th Infantry in World War II. Washington, D.C.: U.S. Army Center of Military History, 1999.

National Register of Historic Places Nomination Form: Camp Naco. National Park Service, July 9, 2010.

Sheire, James, and Robert V. Simmonds. *Historic Structure Report: Castolon Army Compound, Big Bend National Park, Texas.* Denver, CO: Denver Service Center Historic Preservation Team, 1973. https://npshistory.com/ publications/bibe/hsr-castolon-army-compound.pdf.

Newspapers and Periodicals

Arizona Gleam (Phoenix).
Arizona Republican (Phoenix).
Arizona Silver Belt (Globe, AZ).
Arizona Sun (Phoenix).
Arizona Weekly Citizen (Tucson).
Arizona Weekly Journal-Miner/Weekly Arizona Miner (Prescott).
Arkansas Mansion (Little Rock).
Army and Navy Journal.
Army and Navy Register.
Border Vidette (Nogales, AZ).
Chicago Defender.
Clifton Clarion.
Coolidge Examiner.
Daily Optic (Las Vegas, NM).
Daily Review (Bisbee, AZ).
Daily Tombstone.
Evening Star (Washington, D.C.).
Graham Guardian (Safford, AZ).
Harper's Weekly.
Michigan Chronicle (Detroit).
Mohave County Miner (Mineral Park, AZ).
New York Age.
New York Daily Tribune.
New York Freeman.
New York Globe.
New York Sun.
New York Times.

Nogales International.
Oasis (Arizola, AZ).
Oasis (Nogales, AZ).
Phoenix Index.
Phoenix Tribune.
Phoenix Weekly Herald.
Prescott Weekly Courier.
St. Johns Herald (AZ).
Winslow Mail.

Published Works

Alexander, David V. *Arizona Frontier Military Place Names, 1846–1912.* Las Cruces, NM: Yucca Tree Press, 2002.

Ball, Larry D. *Ambush at Bloody Run: The Wham Payroll Robbery of 1889— A Story of Politics, Religion, Race, and Banditry in Arizona.* Tucson: Arizona Historical Society, 2000.

Baumler, Mark F. *The Archeology of Faraway Ranch Arizona: Prehistoric, Historic, and 20th Century.* Tucson, AZ: Western Archeological and Conservation Center, 1984.

Bigelow, John, Jr. *On the Bloody Trail of Geronimo.* Tucson, AZ: Westernlore Press, 1986.

Bolton, Charles C. *Home Front Battles: World War II Mob Mobilization and Race in the Deep South.* Oxford, UK: Oxford University Press, 2024.

Brandes, Ray. *Frontier Military Posts of Arizona.* Globe, AZ: Dale Stuart King, 1960.

Creamer, Robert W. *Stengel: His Life and Times.* New York: Simon and Schuster, 1984.

Dinges, Bruce J. "Leighton Finley A Forgotten Soldier of the Apache Wars." *Journal of Arizona History* 29, no. 2 (Summer 1988): 163–84.

Dobak, William A., and Thomas D. Phillips. *The Black Regulars, 1866–1898.* Norman: University of Oklahoma Press, 2001.

Eisenhower, John S.D. *Intervention!: The United States and the Mexican Revolution, 1913–1917.* New York: W.W. Norton & Company, 1995.

Finley, James P. "The Buffalo Soldiers at Fort Huachuca." *Huachuca Illustrated: A Magazine of the Fort Huachuca Museum* 1 (1993): 42–77.

———. "The Buffalo Soldiers at Fort Huachuca." *Huachuca Illustrated: A Magazine of the Fort Huachuca Museum* 2 (1996): 1–4, 9–19.

Fletcher, Marvin E. *American's First Black General: Benjamin O. Davis, Sr., 1880–1970*. Lawrence: University Press of Kansas, 1989.

Gale, Jack C. "Lebo in Pursuit." *Journal of Arizona History* 21, no. 1 (Spring 1980): 11–24.

Glass, E.L.N., comp. and ed. *The History of the Tenth Cavalry, 1866–1921*. Fort Collins, CO: Army Press, 1972.

Hardaway, Roge D. "Unlawful Love: A History of Arizona's Miscegenation Law." *Journal of Arizona History* 27, no. 4 (Winter 1986): 377–90.

Hargrove, Hondon B. *Buffalo Soldiers in Italy: Black Americans in World War II*. Jefferson, NC: McFarland, circa 1985.

Harris, Theodore D., ed. and comp. *Henry O. Flipper, Black Frontiersman: The Memoirs of Henry O. Flipper, First Black Graduate of West Point*. Fort Worth: Texas Christian University Press, 1997.

Hooker, Forrestine C. *When Geronimo Rode*. Garden City, NY: Doubleday, Page & Company, 1924.

Horne, Gerald. *Black and Brown: African Americans and the Mexican Revolution, 1910–1920*. New York: New York University Press, 2005.

Huachuca Illustrated: A Magazine of the Fort Huachuca Museum 9. "World War II at Huachuca, 1940–1949" (1999): 7–165.

Jefferson, Robert F. *Fighting For Hope: African American Troops of the 93rd Infantry Division in World War II and Postwar America*. Baltimore, MD: Johns Hopkins University Press, 2008.

Johnson, Jesse J. *A Pictorial History of Black Soldiers (1619–1969) in Peace and War*. Hampton, VA: Hampton Institute, 1969.

Kenner, Charles L. *Buffalo Soldiers and Officers of the Ninth Cavalry, 1867–1898*. Norman: University of Oklahoma Press, 1999.

Kühn, Brandt. *Chronicles of War: Apache & Yavapai Resistance in the Southwestern United States and Northern Mexico, 1821–1937*. Tucson: Arizona Historical Society, 2014.

Lamm, Alan K. *Five Black Preachers in Army Blue, 1884–1901: The Buffalo Soldier Chaplains*. Lewiston, NY: Mellen Press, 1998.

Lane, Ann J. *The Brownsville Affair: National Crisis and Black Reaction*. Port Washington, NY: Kennikat Press, 1971.

Langellier, John P. *Scouting with the Buffalo Soldiers: Lieutenant Powhattan Clarke, Frederic Remington, and the Tenth Cavalry in in the Southwest*. Denton: University of North Texas Press, 2020.

———. *Southern Arizona Military Outposts*. Charleston, SC: Arcadia Publishing, 2011.

———. "The Tenth U.S. Cavalry in Prescott, A.T." *Territorial Times Prescott Arizona Corral of Westerners International* 1 (November 2009): 22–29.

Langellier, John P., and Alan M. Osur. *Chaplain Allen Allensworth and the Twenty-Fourth Infantry, 1886–1906*. Tucson, AZ: Tucson Corral of the Westerners, 1980.

Lee, Ulysses. *The Employment of Negro Troops*. Washington, D.C.: Office of the Chief of Military History U.S. Army, 1966.

Leiker, James N. *Racial Borders: Black Soldiers Along the Rio Grande*. College Station: Texas A&M Press, 2002.

Louisa, Angelo J., ed. *The African American Baseball Experience in Nebraska: Essays and Memories*. Jefferson, NC: McFarland and Company, 2021.

MacGregor, Morris J., Jr. *Integration of the Armed Forces, 1940–1965*. Washington, D.C.: United States Army Center of Military History, 2001.

Malloy, Jerry. "The 25th Infantry Regiment Takes the Field." *National Pastime* 15 (1995).

Marriott, Barbara. *Annie's Guests: Tales from a Frontier Hotel*. Tucson, AZ: Catymatt Productions, 2000.

Matthews, Matt M. *The U.S. Army on the Mexican Border: A Historical Perspective*. Fort Leavenworth, KS: Combat Studies Institute Press, 2007.

Morehouse, Maggi M. *Fighting in the Jim Crow Army: Black Men and Women Remember World War II*. Lanham, MD: Rowman & Littlefield Publishers Inc., 2000.

Motley, Mary Penick. *The Invisible Soldier: The Experience of the Black Soldier, World War II*. Detroit, MI: Wayne State University Press, 1975.

Muller, William G. *Twenty-Fourth Infantry Past and Present a Brief History of the Regiment Compiled from Official Records, Under the Direction of the Regimental Commander*. N.p., 1923.

Nalty, Bernard C. *Strength for the Fight: A History of Black Americans in the Military*. New York: Free Press, 1986.

Nankivell, John Henry. *History of the Twenty-Fifth Regiment, United States Infantry, 1866–1926*. Denver, CO: Smith-Brooks Printing, 1926.

Nash, Horace D. "Community Building on the Border: The Role of the 24th Infantry Band at Columbus, New Mexico, 1916–1922." *Fort Concho and the South Plains Journal* 2, no. 3 (Summer 1990): 76–92.

Nearing, Richard, and David Hoff. *Arizona Military Installations: Presidios, Camps & Forts, 1752–1922*. Tempe, AZ: Gem Publishing Company, 1998.

Peretz, Pauline. *Une Armée Noire: Fort Huachuca, Arizona (1941–1945)*. Paris: Éditions du Seuil, 2022.

Phillips, Tom. "Sobriquet: A Chronological Commentary on the Name 'Buffalo Soldier.'" *Journal of America's Military Past* 35, no. 2 (Spring/Summer 2010): 5–30.

Radbourne, Allan. *Corporal Edward Scott, Frontier Cavalryman*. London: English Westerners' Society, 2014.

Remington, Frederic. "A Scout with the Buffalo Soldiers." *Century* 37 (April 1889): 899–912.

Rives, Timothy, and Robert Rives. "The Booker T Four's Unlikely Journey from Prison Baseball to the Negro Leagues." *Prologue* 36, no. 2 (Summer 2004): 20–29.

Rodney, George Brydges. *As a Cavalryman Remembers*. Caldwell, ID: Caxton Printers Ltd., 1944.

Rolak, Bruno J. *History of Fort Huachuca, Arizona*. El Paso, TX: Southwest Antiquarians, 1972.

Schubert, Frank N. *Black Valor: Buffalo Soldiers and the Medal of Honor, 1870–1898*. Wilmington, DE: Scholarly Resources, 1998.

———. "Buffalo Soldiers: Myths and Realities." *Army History: The Professional Bulletin of Army History* 52 (Spring 2001): 13–18.

———. *On the Trail of the Buffalo Soldier: Biographies of African Americans in the U.S. Army, 1866–1917*. Wilmington, DE: Scholarly Resources, 1995.

Schubert, Irene, and Frank N. Schubert. *On the Trail of the Buffalo Soldiers: New and Revised Biographies of African-Americans in the U.S. Army, 1866–1917*. Lanham, MD: Scarecrow Press, 2004.

Smith, Cornelius C., Jr. *Fort Huachuca: The Story of a Frontier Post*. Fort Huachuca, AZ: Department of the Army, 1981.

Smith, Gloria L. *Black Americana in Arizona*. Tucson, AZ: Gloria L. Smith, 1977.

Smith, Steven D. *The African American Soldier at Fort Huachuca, Arizona, 1892–1946*. Seattle, WA: U.S. Army Corps of Engineer, 2001.

Smith, Steven D., and James A. Zeidler, eds. *A Historic Context for the African American Military Experience*. Champaign, IL: U.S. Army Construction Engineering Research Laboratories, 1998.

Stern, Ray. "1942 Phoenix Thanksgiving Day Riot." *Phoenix New Times*, November 25, 2020.

Tagg, Martin D. *The Camp at Bonita Cañon: A Buffalo Soldier Camp in Chiricahua National Monument Arizona*. Tucson, AZ: Western Archeological and Conservation Center, 1987.

Voogd, Jan. *Race & Resistance: The Red Summer of 1919*. New York: Peter Lang, 2008.

Wharfield, H.B. *10th Cavalry & Border Fights*. El Cajon, CA: Wharfield, 1965.
————. *With Scouts and Cavalry at Fort Apache*. Tucson: Arizona Pioneers' Historical Society, 1965.
Wilson, Steve, ed. *Child of the Fighting Tenth: On the Frontier with the Buffalo Soldiers Forrestine C. Hooker*. Oxford, UK: Oxford University Press, 2003.
Work, David K. "Enforcing Neutrality: The Tenth U.S. Cavalry on the Mexican Border, 1913–1919." *Western Historical Quarterly* 40, no. 2 (Summer 2009): 179–200.
————. "THEIR LIFE'S BLOOD: The Tenth Cavalry in Arizona, 1914–1921." *Journal of Arizona History* 46, no. 4 (Winter 2006): 349–74.

Electronic Sources

Lee, Ulysses. "The Employment of Negro Troops." U.S. Army Center of Military History. https://history.army.mil/html/books/011/11-4/CMH_Pub_11-4-1.pdf.
Library of Congress. "NAACP: A Century in the Fight for Freedom." https://www.loc.gov/exhibits/naacp/the-new-negro-movement.html?loclr-blogpoe.
MacGregor, Morris J., Jr. "Integration of the Armed Forces, 1940–1965." Defense Studies Series. U.S. Army Center of Military History. https://history.army.mil/html/books/050/50-1-1/cmhPub_50-1-1.pdf.
Matthews, Matt M. "The US Army on the Mexican Border: A Historical Perspective." Army University Press. https://www.armyupress.army.mil/Portals/7/combat-studies-institute/csi-books/Matthews_op22.pdf.
Nogales Buffalo Soldiers. www.NogalesBuffaloSoldiers.org.
Schubert, Frank N. "Buffalo Soldiers: Myths and Realities." *Army History*, no. 52 (Spring 2001): 13–18. JSTOR. https://www.jstor.org/stable/26305152.
Smith, Steven D. *The African American Soldier at Fort Huachuca, Arizona, 1892–1946*. Columbia: University of South Carolina–Columbia, University Libraries, 2001. https://scholarcommons.sc.edu/anth_facpub/55.
Smith, Steven D., and James A. Zeidler. "A Historic Context for the African American Military Experience." Defense Technical Information Center. https://apps.dtic.mil/sti/citations/ADA350395.

Unpublished and Miscellaneous Sources

Arizona State Board of Health, Bureau of Vital Statistics. Original Certificate of Death State Index No. 152.

Baumler, Mark F., and Richard V.H Ahlstrom. "The Garfield Monument: An 1886 Memorial to the Buffalo Soldiers in Arizona." Manuscript. Western Archeological and Conservation Center, NPS, Tucson, 1986.

Corbusier, William T. Interview. Arizona Historical Society, Tucson, October 1968.

Hamilton, George F. "History of the Ninth Regiment U.S. Cavalry." Manuscript. U.S. Army Heritage and Education Center, Carlisle Barracks, Pennsylvania, n.d.

Harris, Theodore Delano. "Henry Ossian Flipper: The First Black Graduate of West Point." PhD dissertation, University of Minnesota, 1971.

Jackson-Houston, Donna. E-mail to the author, July 12, 2024. Subject: "Lucius Franklin Monroe Jackson—25th Infantry, Nogales Family Bio."

Lee, R.V. Official State of Military Service and Death of Louis A. Carter Service, Number O4358, Louis A. Carter File, Fort Huachuca Museum, Arizona.

Marchbank, Vance Hunter, Sr. "Forty Years in the Army." Unpublished manuscript, circa 1940. Transcription. Fort Huachuca Museum, 2006.

Potts, Benjamin Franklin. Biographical File, Fort Verde State Park, Camp Verde, Arizona.

Remington, Frederic. "Journal of a Trip Across the Continent through Arizona and Sonora Old Mexico." Topeka, Kansas State Historical Society.

Riggs, Lilian Erickson. Letter to National Park Service Volunteer-in-Parks Richard Murray, February 1966. Western Archaeological and Conservation Center, NPS, Tucson, Arizona.

Suydam Cowley, Nellie. Letters, 1912–27. Author's collection.

Torres, Louis, and Mark Baumler. "A History of the Buildings and Structures of the Faraway Ranch, Historic Structures Report, Historical and Archaeological Data Section." Manuscript, Western Archeological and Conservation Center, Tucson, 1984.

Valentin, Edward. "Black Enlisted Men in the U.S.-Mexico Border: Race, Citizenship, and Military Occupation, 1866–1930." PhD dissertation, Rice University, Houston, Texas, 2020.

William Neal Collection, 1849–1936. MS 579. Arizona Historical Society Library, Tucson.

Work, David K. "The Fighting Tenth Cavalry: Black Soldiers in the United States Army, 1892–1918." MA thesis, Oklahoma State University, 1998.

Wynn, Neil Alan. "The Afro-American and the Second World War." PhD dissertation, The Open University, 1973.

Yancy, James Walter. "The Negro of Tucson, Past, and the Negro of Tucson, Past and Present." MA thesis, University of Arizona, 1933.

ABOUT THE AUTHOR

J ohn P. Langellier received his BA and MA in history and historical archaeology from the University of San Diego and a PhD from Kansas State University with a concentration on U.S. military history. His career spans more than five decades in various public history positions. Langellier has written, cowritten and/or edited scores of articles, as well as dozens of books and monographs, including *More Work than Glory: A History of the Buffalo Soldiers, 1866–1916* and the Arcadia Images of America series title *Southern Arizona Military Outposts*. He also has worked in motion picture and TV productions, including on features and documentaries; leads military history tours; and frequently appears as a public speaker on an array of historical topics.